ALGEBRA

EQUATIONS AND EXPRESSIONS

Walker Maths Essentials: Algebra 5+
1st Edition
Charlotte Walker
Victoria Walker

Designer: Cheryl Smith, Macarn Design
Production controller: Magda Koralewska

Acknowledgements
Cover photo courtesy of Shutterstock.

We wish to thank the Boards of Trustees of Darfield and Riccarton High Schools for allowing us to use materials and ideas developed while teaching. Our thanks also go to all past and present colleagues, especially Kath Wilson, who have generously shared their experience and ideas.

For product information and technology assistance,
in Australia call **1300 790 853**;
in New Zealand call **0800 449 725**

For permission to use material from this text or product, please email **aust.permissions@cengage.com**

National Library of New Zealand Cataloguing-in-Publication Data
A catalogue record for this book is available from the National Library of New Zealand.

978 0 17 044709 6

Cengage Learning Australia
Level 7, 80 Dorcas Street
South Melbourne, Victoria Australia 3205

Cengage Learning New Zealand
Unit 4B Rosedale Office Park
331 Rosedale Road, Albany, North Shore 0632, NZ

For learning solutions, visit **cengage.co.nz**

Printed in China by 1010 Printing International Limited.
5 6 7 24

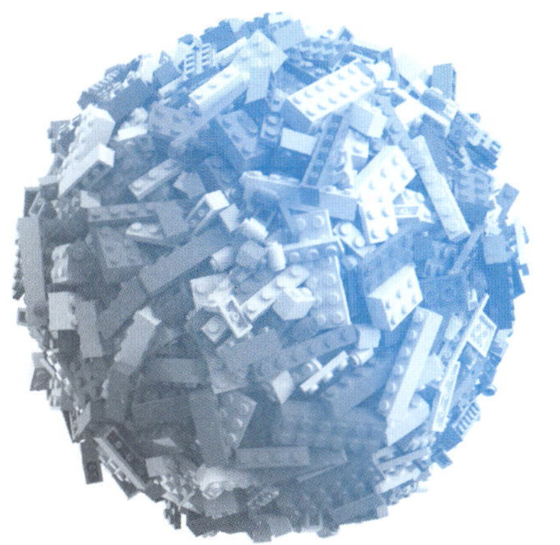

CONTENTS

ISBN: 9780170447096

Glossary

Make your own glossary of key terms:

Term	Definition	Picture/Example
Expression		
Term		
Like terms		
Constant		
Power		
Index (plural: indices)		
Exponent		
Variable		
Coefficient		
Expand		
Factorise		
Solve		

ISBN: 9780170447096

Term	Definition	Picture/Example
Simplify		
Substitute		
Evaluate		
Product		
Sum		
Reciprocal		
Highest common factor (HCF)		
Numerator		
Denominator		
Dimensions		
Exponential		
Simultaneous		

ISBN: 9780170447096

Revision

Simplifying expressions

Multiplying

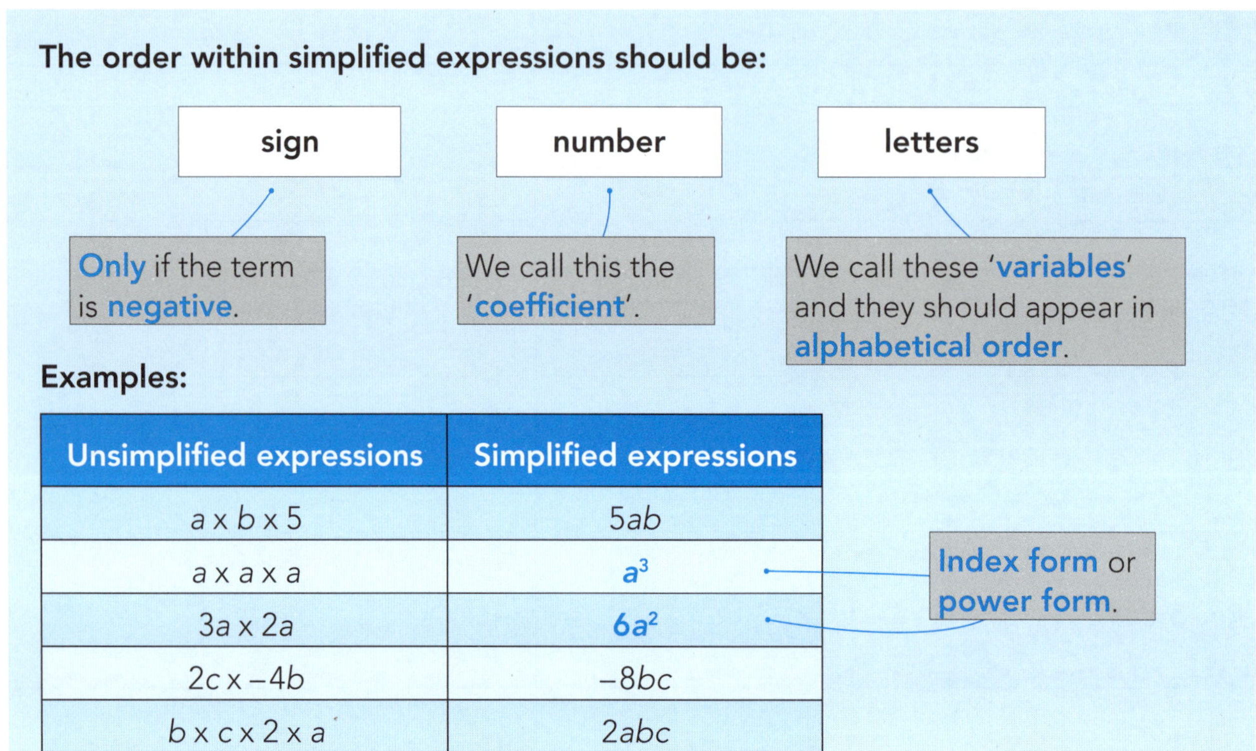

The order within simplified expressions should be:

Examples:

Unsimplified expressions	Simplified expressions
$a \times b \times 5$	$5ab$
$a \times a \times a$	a^3
$3a \times 2a$	$6a^2$
$2c \times -4b$	$-8bc$
$b \times c \times 2 \times a$	$2abc$

Simplify the following expressions.

1 $p \times p =$ ____________

2 $h \times g \times m =$ ____________

3 $4 \times c =$ ____________

4 $3f \times 4g =$ ____________

5 $-5 \times w =$ ____________

6 $f \times -g \times -9 =$ ____________

Dividing

- 'x divided by y' can be written as either $x \div y$ or $\frac{x}{y}$.

Example:

$$\frac{12b}{3} = \frac{4b}{1} \times \frac{3}{3}$$

$$= 4b$$

Remember:

1 $\frac{\text{anything}}{1}$ = itself e.g. $\frac{4b}{1} = 4b$

2 $\frac{\text{anything}}{\text{itself}} = 1$ e.g. $\frac{3}{3} = 1$

ISBN: 9780170447096

More examples:

Unsimplified expressions	Simplified expressions
$a \div 4$	$\frac{a}{4}$ or $\frac{1}{4}a$
$6 \div a$	$\frac{6}{a}$
$\frac{2a}{4}$	$\frac{a}{2}$ or $\frac{1}{2}a$
$\frac{9b}{3a}$	$\frac{3b}{a}$

Simplify the following expressions.

7 $6g \div 3 =$ ________________

8 $15p \div 3n =$ ________________

9 $20 \div 5f =$ ________________

10 $12ef \div 3e =$ ________________

11 $\frac{18c}{6} =$ ________________

12 $\frac{7}{14g} =$ ________________

Putting it together

Simplify the following expressions.

1 $\frac{3b}{6} =$ ________________

2 $5a \times 4 =$ ________________

3 $\frac{2}{16d} =$ ________________

4 $p \times 4 \times q =$ ________________

5 $2 \times m \times 5 \times n =$ ________________

6 $\frac{9}{3e} =$ ________________

7 $8a \div 4 =$ ________________

8 $3 \times -4b =$ ________________

9 $j \times 7k =$ ________________

10 $7 \div a =$ ________________

Like terms

- Terms can only be added or subtracted if they are '**like**' terms.
- 'Like' terms must have exactly the **same variables**, and each variable must be raised to exactly the **same power**.
- Order does not matter.
- The sign does not matter.

Examples: The following **are** like terms: ab, $2ab$, ba, $-ab$.

The following are **not** like terms:

a^2b^3 and a^2b^5 — The b is to the power of **5**, not **3**.

a^2b^3 and b^3a^2c — Includes a '**c**' term.

Join the dots to match each term on the left with the like term on the right.

$3p^2$ •	• $9qp^2$
$7qp$ •	• p^2qr
$6p^2qr^2$ •	• $-pq$
rp^2q •	• p^2r^2q
pqr^2 •	• $80q^2p$
$-pq^2$ •	• $-7rp^2q^2$
$-4p^2q^2r$ •	• $10pqr$
$-p^2q$ •	• $-q^2r^2p$
$2pq^2r^2$ •	• $-3r^2pq$
$-qpr$ •	• $-7p^2$

 ISBN: 9780170447096

Adding and subtracting

- When adding or subtracting, you can **combine only like terms**.
- Only the ones with **exactly** the same variables and powers can be combined.

Hint: It is helpful to circle, underline or highlight terms that are 'like' each other with the same shape or colour.

Examples: Simplify these.

1 $5a + 2b - a = 4a + 2b$

$5a$ and $-a$ are like terms, so they can be combined $\Rightarrow$ $4a$.

2 $7p^2 - 4q + 9p + p^2 + q = 8p^2 - 3q + 9p$

$7p^2$ and $+p^2$ are like terms, so they can be combined $\Rightarrow$ $8p^2$.
$-4q$ and $+q$ are like terms, so they can be combined $\Rightarrow$ $-3q$.

Simplify these by adding or subtracting like terms.

1 $y + y + y + y =$ ____________

2 $4a + a + 5a =$ ____________

3 $9x - 3x + x + x =$ ____________

4 $10y + y - 5y - 2y =$ ____________

5 $5y + x + y =$ ____________

6 $2 + x + 1 =$ ____________

7 $6y + x - 3x =$ ____________

8 $4m + n + 3m =$ ____________

9 $7x + 3y - 5x + 2 =$ ____________

10 $5p + 7q - 2p - 3q + 11 =$ ____________

11 $5a - a + 6b + b =$ ____________

12 $10x + 4 - 3x - 1 =$ ____________

13 $6f - 2g - 7f - 12g - g =$ ____________

14 $p + p^2 + 2p =$ ____________

15 $13x^2 + 7 - x - 2x + x^2 =$ ____________

16 $2p^2 + 10 - 3q^2 - p^2 =$ ____________

ISBN: 9780170447096

Mixing it up

Simplify the following.

1 $k \div 4k =$ ______________

2 $7fg + 4g - 13gf - fg =$ ______________

3 $\frac{18cd}{6c} =$ ______________

4 $-p \times 6 \times q \times (-2qp) =$ ______________

5 $x^2 + 7x - 1 - x + 3x^2 =$ ______________

6 $\frac{7x}{21xy} =$ ______________

7 $8ab - b - 2b^2 - ba - 3b =$ ______________

8 $\frac{wxyz}{5wyz} =$ ______________

9 $\frac{6a}{12} =$ ______________

10 $-z + z^2 + 2yz - 3z^2 =$ ______________

11 $f \times 2 \times 5g \times 3f \times g =$ ______________

12 $\frac{25mn}{45mn} =$ ______________

13 $abc \div 5b =$ ______________

14 $5p^2 - 4p - p^2 - 1 - p =$ ______________

15 $-\frac{12nm}{3n} =$ ______________

16 $m \times 2n \times 5 \div 4 =$ ______________

17 $pq^2 + 3pq - q^2p - qp =$ ______________

18 $-cd \times 4 \times (-c) \times 2 =$ ______________

19 $ab \div 7bc =$ ______________

20 $a + ab^2 - 2b + b^2 - b + 9a =$ ______________

ISBN: 9780170447096

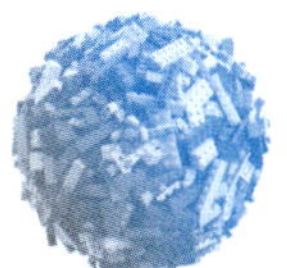

The language of algebra

Words to operations

Write down the most appropriate operation (**+**, **−**, **x** or **÷**) for each of the following terms. You do **not** need to write down the answers.

	Terms	Operation
1	What is twelve **more than** ten?	+
2	Find **the sum** of thirty-five and fifty.	
3	Calculate four **times** nine.	
4	Find the result when eighteen is **reduced by** six.	
5	What is the **product** of seven and eleven?	
6	Calculate four **less than** thirteen.	
7	What is twenty **take away** eight?	
8	Find thirty-two **divided by** four.	
9	What is fifteen **decreased by** nine?	
10	If twenty lollies are **shared between** five friends, how many does each get?	
11	Find the **difference between** twenty-two and fifty.	
12	What is seventeen **plus** four?	
13	Find a quarter **of** sixty.	
14	Fourteen is **subtracted from** thirty.	
15	Find twenty-eight **and** sixteen.	
16	Eleven is **added** to eight.	
17	Find a number which is three **smaller than** two.	
18	What is the **total of** nineteen and twelve?	
19	Calculate the result when thirteen is **multiplied by** nine.	
20	What is fifteen **increased by** four?	

Phrases to expressions

- In algebra we use **operations** along with **variables** and numbers to write **expressions**.
- A **variable** is represented by a **letter of the alphabet**, which may be the initial of what it represents, e.g d for **d**istance.
- **Brackets** are used to indicate which operations should be done **first**.
- Notice the positions of **commas** — they can also indicate which operation should be done first.

Some tricks:

- We do not write in the times sign between a number and a variable, e.g. $2d$ means $2 \times d$.
- We do not write an exponent for powers of one, e.g. d^1 is written as d.
- We do not write a coefficent if it is 1, e.g. $1d = d$.

Some special terms:

Double or twice d	$2 \times d$ or $2d$
Treble or triple d	$3 \times d$ or $3d$
Half of d	$\frac{1}{2} \times d$ or $d \div 2$ or $\frac{1}{2}d$ or $\frac{d}{2}$
Quarter of d	$\frac{d}{4}$ or $\frac{1}{4}d$

Note that $2 \times d = d \times 2$, but we write the **number first**: $2d$.

Remember that order doesn't matter when we add, so we can write $2b + 10$ or $10 + 2b$.

Examples:

Phrase	Operation	Variable	Expression
10 more than twice b	+ and x	b	$2b + 10$ or $10 + 2b$
Five times a total of d and 3	x and +	d	$5(d + 3)$
Triple the difference between m and 6	x and –	m	$3(m - 6)$
p shared between two, reduced by 7	÷ and –	p	$\frac{p}{2} - 7$

The comma means you do the sharing **first**, and **then** reduce by 7.

 ISBN: 9780170447096

Match the phrases below with the correct expression from the box below.

$2c^2$	$4^2 - b$	$(4 - b)^2$	$\frac{b}{3} - 4$
$\frac{b-4}{3}$	$4(b + 2)$	$b^2 - 4$	$2(b - 4)$
$4 + \frac{b}{2}$	$2b - 4$	$3(b + c)$	$(b - 4)^2$
$4b + 2$	$b + 3c$	$(2c)^2$	$\frac{4 + b}{2}$

	Phrase	Expression
1	Four times b plus 2	
2	Double the difference between b and 4	
3	A total of b and triple c	
4	Four plus half b	
5	The square of four less than b	
6	Twice c, squared	
7	Half of the sum of four and b	
8	Four less than twice b	
9	The square of four, reduced by b	
10	The square of four reduced by b	
11	A third of four less than b	
12	Triple the total of b and c	
13	A third of b, decreased by four	
14	Four less than b squared	
15	Quadruple the sum of b and two	
16	Twice the square of c	

ISBN: 9780170447096

Write an expression for these phrases. Use the variable *y*. Some expressions could be interpreted in two ways. If so, write both answers.

17 Triple a term with seven added to it

18 Triple a term, with seven added to it

19 Three less than a variable divided by four

20 Three less than a variable, divided by four

21 Half a variable plus three

22 Half a variable, plus three

23 Nine less than a double a number

24 The square of the difference between nine and a number

Write a phrase for these expressions.

25 $2b + 7$

26 $2(b + 7)$

27 $5 - b \div 3$

28 $\frac{5 - b}{3}$

29 $\frac{b}{4} + 7$

30 $\frac{b + 7}{4}$

31 $(7 - b)^2$

32 $7 - b^2$

 ISBN: 9780170447096

More about variables

- We use **letters** of the alphabet to represent **variables**.
- A **variable** is a quantity that **can change**.

Example:
Grandma pays Ruby \$12 per hour to do jobs during the school holidays. She takes the bus to Grandma's house, and the return fare is \$4.

On Monday she worked for **3** hours.	She earns \$12 x **3** – 4 = \$32
On Tuesday she worked for **5** hours.	She earns \$12 x **5** – 4 = \$56
On Friday she worked for **2** hours.	She earns \$12 x **2** – 4 = \$20

We call the number of ***hours*** worked ***h***, so the amount she earns each day is 12***h*** – 4 .

h is called the **variable** and it represents the number of **hours** she works each day. *h* **changes** depending on how long she works each day.

12***h*** – 4 is called an **expression**.

Identify the variable and the expression.

1 Grandma has a jar which contains 47 lollies. Ruby eats two every time she visits. Provided Grandma does not restock the jar, the total remaining in the jar can be given by the expression **Total = 47 – 2v**.

a The variable is ______ and it stands for ________________________________.

b Use the expression to calculate how many lollies would remain after seven visits.

____

2 Ollie needs to calculate the price for producing booklets for members of his sports club. He can get the covers and binding for each booklet for \$3, and it will cost ten cents for each page. The total cost of each booklet can be given by the expression **Total = 3 + 0.1*p***.

a The variable is ______ and it stands for ________________________________.

b Use the expression to calculate how much it will cost to produce a 35-page booklet.

____

3 Mason is building a run for his chickens. He needs six posts for the smallest possible run, and an additional two posts for every metre he adds to its length. He worked out that the number of posts needed was given by the expression **Total = 2*m* + 6**.

a The variable is ______ and it stands for ________________________________.

b Use the expression to calculate how many posts he would need if he adds 5 metres to its length.

____

ISBN: 9780170447096

Powers

The words **power**, **exponent** and **index** all mean the same thing.

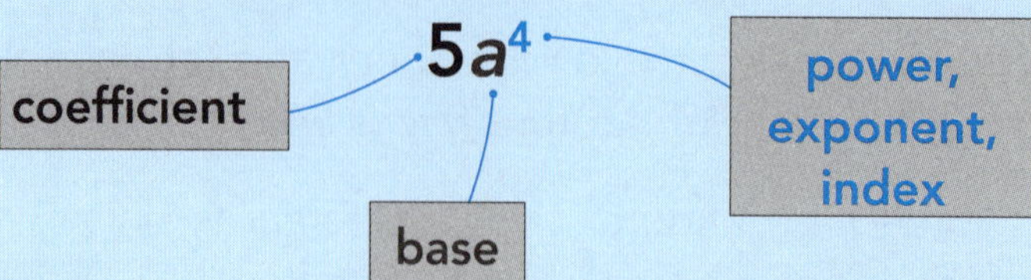

You need to know that:

- a^4 means **a x a x a x a**
- a^1 is the same as **a**
- $a^0 = 1$

This is important but often forgotten. It only works as long as $a \neq 0$.

Multiplying powers

When multiplying, we **add** the indices: $a^n \times a^m = a^{n+m}$

Examples:

1 $a^3 \times a^2 = a \times a \times a \times a \times a$
$= a^5$

$3 + 2 = 5$

If you are not sure, expand each term.

2 $2ab \times 7ab^2 = 2 \times a \times b \times 7 \times a \times b \times b$
$= 14a^2b^3$

3 $3a^4 \times 5a^9 = 15a^{13}$

It helps to deal with the **coefficients** first.

Circle/highlight the correct simplified answer for each of the following.

1	$b^3 \times 2b$	$2b^3$	b^4
		$2b^4$	$3b^4$

2	$2a^2 \times 3a^3$	$6a^5$	$5a^5$
		$5a^6$	$6a^6$

Simplify these.

3 $p^2 \times p \times p =$ ____________

4 $a^2 \times a^7 =$ ____________

5 $b^3 \times b^0 =$ ____________

6 $e^2f^3 \times e^4f =$ ____________

7 $a^0 \times 2a^0 =$ ____________

8 $2ab^5 \times 4a^3b =$ ____________

9 $3p^2 \times 5p^3 \times 2p^0 =$ ____________

10 $2ab^2 \times 4a^3b \times 3abc =$ ____________

 ISBN: 9780170447096

Dividing powers

When dividing, we **subtract** the indices: $a^n \div a^m = a^{n-m}$

Examples:

1 $a^5 \div a^2 = \dfrac{a \times a \times a \times a \times a}{a \times a}$

$= a^3$ — $5 - 2 = 3$

Once again, if you are not sure, expand each term.

2 $\dfrac{12a^6}{4a^2} = \dfrac{4 \times 3 \times a \times a \times a \times a \times a \times a}{4 \times a \times a}$

$= 3a^4$

Deal with the **coefficients** first.

3 $\dfrac{10a^3}{2a^4} = \dfrac{5 \times 2 \times a \times a \times a}{2 \times a \times a \times a \times a}$

$= \dfrac{5}{a}$

Your answer may have a variable as the denominator.

Circle/highlight the correct simplified answer for each of the following.

1

$\dfrac{12a^{12}}{2a^2}$	$6a^6$	$10a^{10}$
	$10a^6$	$6a^{10}$

2

$\dfrac{2a^2b^6}{6a^8b^2}$	$\dfrac{b^3}{3a^4}$	$\dfrac{b^4}{3a^4}$
	$\dfrac{b^3}{3a^6}$	$\dfrac{b^4}{3a^6}$

Simplify these.

3 $\dfrac{y}{y^4} =$ ____________

4 $\dfrac{15y^{12}}{10y^4} =$ ____________

5 $\dfrac{x^6y^8}{x^3y^2} =$ ____________

6 $\dfrac{7ef^3}{21e^2f^2} =$ ____________

7 $\dfrac{2p^5q^5}{6p^4q^6} =$ ____________

8 $\dfrac{16x^0y^2}{20x^3y^{10}} =$ ____________

ISBN: 9780170447096

Powers of powers

When finding a power of a power, we **multiply** the indices: $(a^n)^m = a^{n \times m}$

Examples: **1** $(a^5)^2 = (a \times a \times a \times a \times a) \times (a \times a \times a \times a \times a)$
$= a^{10}$

5 x 2 = 10

Once again, if you are not sure, expand each term.

2 $(2a^3)^3 = (2 \times a \times a \times a) \times (2 \times a \times a \times a) \times (2 \times a \times a \times a)$
$= 8a^9$

Deal with the **coefficient** first: $2^3 = 8$.

Circle/highlight the correct simplified answer for each of the following.

1

$(5f^4)^2$	$25f^6$	$25f^8$
	$10f^6$	$10f^8$

2

$(3y^{10}z^4)^2$	$9y^{12}z^6$	$9y^{12}z^8$
	$9y^{20}z^6$	$9y^{20}z^8$

Simplify these.

3 $(2b^5)^3 =$ ______________

4 $(a^8)^0 =$ ______________

5 $(4x^3y)^2 =$ ______________

6 $(5x^2y^4)^3 =$ ______________

7 $7(a^3bc^5)^2 =$ ______________

8 $5(2p^4q^2)^3 =$ ______________

9 $(3(5p^2q)^2)^0 =$ ______________

10 $(3(2d^3e^4)^3)^2 =$ ______________

11 $(7a^3(5ab)^0)^2 =$ ______________

12 $(p^2(2pq^2)^3)^2 =$ ______________

 ISBN: 9780170447096

Mixing it up

Simplify the following.

1 $2c^{10} \times c^2 =$ ______

2 $d^{20} \div d^4 =$ ______

3 $(y^5)^2 =$ ______

4 $\frac{3p^{12}}{p^4} =$ ______

5 $\frac{c}{c^7} =$ ______

6 $(p^6)^0 =$ ______

7 $e^{11} \times e =$ ______

8 $(2g^3)^4 =$ ______

9 $(6s^3)^2 \div 9s =$ ______

10 $\frac{18g^4 \times 2g}{4g^3} =$ ______

11 $\frac{3p \times 2p^5}{(p^3)^2} =$ ______

______

12 $\frac{(4z^3)^0}{2z} =$ ______

______

13 $(d^2e^5)^2 \div d^2e^{11} =$ ______

14 $a^3b^5 \times ab^4 \div a^3b =$ ______

15 $2(3p^2q^5)^3 =$ ______

______

16 $\frac{36(p^5)^3}{(2p^3)^2} =$ ______

______

Write the following expressions in as many different ways as you can. The first one has been started for you. Check your answers with your neighbour or your teacher.

17 b^{12} $(b^6)^2$, $\frac{b^{13}}{b}$, $b^7 \times b^5$ ______

18 $9y^8$ ______

19 g^6h^4 ______

ISBN: 9780170447096

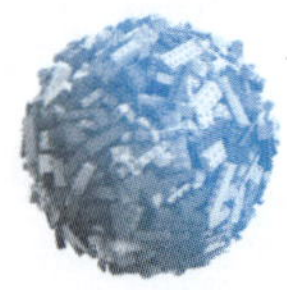

Challenge 1

1 The sides of a rectangle are $3b^2$ and $2b$. Write and simplify an expression for its area.

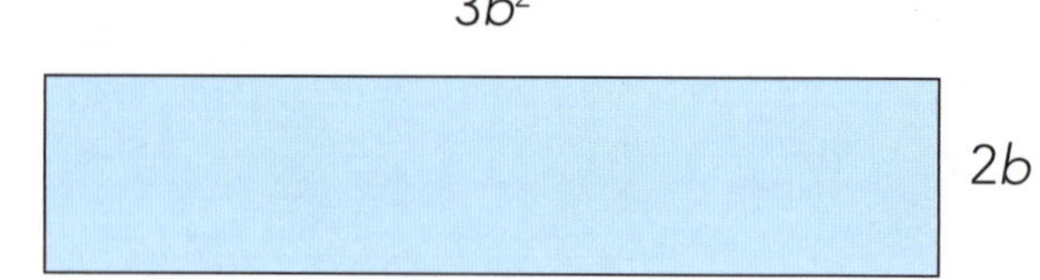

$A =$ ______________________

____

2 A square has sides of $5d^2$. Write and simplify an expression for its area.

$A =$ ______________________

____

3 A rectangle has an area given by the expression $12a^2b^5$. If the length of one side is $3ab^2$, write and simplify an expression for the length of the other side.

$L =$ ______________________

____

4 If the area of a square is $16a^2b^6$, write an expression for the length of one side.

$L =$ ______________________

____

5 The base of a triangle has the length $6pq$, and its perpendicular height is $3p^2$. Write and simplify an expression for its area.

$A =$ ______________________

____

6 The area of a triangle can be written as $3ab^2c^2$. If its base can be written as $6ab$, find an expression for its perpendicular height.

$H =$ ______________________

____

7 Each edge of a cube has a length given by the expression $5d^3$.

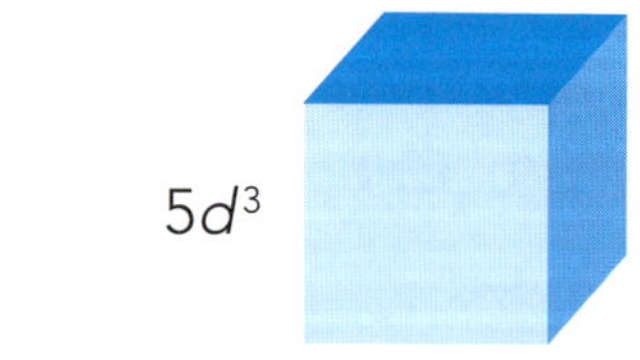

a Write and simplify an expression for its volume.

$V =$ ______________________

____

b Write and simplify an expression for its surface area.

$SA =$ ______________________

____

 ISBN: 9780170447096

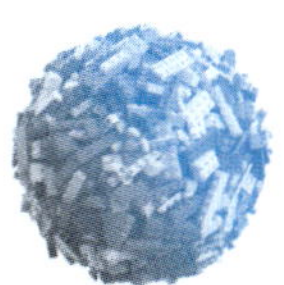

Challenge 2

Join the dots to match each term on the left with the simplified term on the right.

$(4ab^2)^2 \times 2a^2b \times (a^3b)^0$ •	• $\frac{b^3}{3a^2}$
$\frac{12b^4c^2}{4b(3ac)^2}$ •	• $32a^5b^4$
$\frac{ab^3}{(3ab)^2} \times \frac{3ab}{a^3}$ •	• $\frac{b^2}{3a^3}$
$\frac{(6a)^2b^8}{12a^4b^5}$ •	• $\frac{3b^3}{a^2}$
$\frac{(3a^6)^2}{(a^2)^5} - \frac{5(a^3)^4}{a^{10}}$ •	• $4a^3$
$\frac{2a \times a^5 \times (4a^2)^2}{(2a^2)^3}$ •	• $32a^4b^5$
$\frac{9a^3 - 3a^3}{a^2} - \frac{(2ab)^2}{2ab^2}$ •	• $4a^4$
$\frac{3(ab^2)^2c}{a^5b^2c}$ •	• $4a^2$
$28a^3 \times \frac{a^6}{7(a^3)^2}$ •	• $\frac{3b^2}{a^3}$
$\frac{(4a)^3 \times (2b^3)^2 \times (ab^2)^2}{(2b^2)^3}$ •	• $4a$

ISBN: 9780170447096

Find the errors

Some of the following statements are correct and some are incorrect. If the statement is correct, put a tick in the ✓/✗ column. If it is incorrect, put a cross in the ✓/✗ column, explain the error, and write the correct solution.

		✓/✗	Explanation	Correct solution
1	$d^3 \times d^2 \times d^0 = d^6$			
2	$4m^2 + m^2 - m = 5m^4 - m$			
3	$(2h^3)^4 = 16h^{12}$			
4	$6a^2 \times 9a^5 = 54a^7$			
5	$15s^4t^{12} \div 3s^2t^4 = 5s^2t^3$			
6	$3y^3z^7 \times 4y^4z = 12y^7z^7$			
7	$\frac{8p^6q^4}{2p^2q} = 4p^4q^4$			
8	$(3ab^2c^0)^3 = 27a^3b^6c^3$			
9	$7h^3 + 3h^0 - h^3 = 6h^3 + 3$			
10	$12e^3f^2gh^4 = 12gh^4e^3f^2$			

 ISBN: 9780170447096

Brackets

Expanding

- In algebra, '**expand**' means **multiply** out all the **brackets**.
- After expanding you are expected to **collect the like terms** in order to simplify the expression.

If there is **no sign** between a term and a bracket, it is understood that you should **multiply**.

$2(a + 3) = 2 \times a + 2 \times 3$
$= 2a + 6$

Examples:

1 $4(b - 3 + c) = 4b - 12 + 4c$ — $4 \times b - 4 \times 3 + 4 \times c$

2 $2d(5d - e) = 10d^2 - 2de$ — $2d \times 5d - 2d \times e$

3 $-3p(2p - 5) = -6p^2 + 15p$ — $-3p \times 2p - -3p \times 5$

Remember that the negative of (or times) a negative is a **positive**.

4 $-(g - 2) = -1(g - 2)$
$= -g + 2$
$= 2 - g$

Notice:
1 If there is no number written in front of a bracket, it is understood to be a '**1**'.
2 The outcome of multiplying the bracket by –1 is to reverse the order of the contents.

5 $7m(m - 3) - m(10 + m) = 7m^2 - 21m - 10m - m^2$
$= 6m^2 - 31m$

Often you will need to collect like terms in order to simplify the answer.

ISBN: 9780170447096

Circle/highlight the best expanded and simplified answer for each of the following.

1	$2x(x - 5y + 3)$	$2x^2 - 10x + 6x$ $2x^2 - 10y + 6$ $2x^2 - 10xy + 6$ $2x^2 - 10xy + 6x$	**2**	$-3x(1 - x)$	$3x - 3x^2$ $3x^2 - 3x$ $-3x - 3x^2$ $3x^2 + 3x$
3	$3(y - 4) - 2(5 - 4y)$	$11y - 22$ $-5y - 2$ $-5y - 22$ $11y - 2$	**4**	$-(x - 2)$	$x - 2$ $2 - x$ $-x - 2$ $-2 + x$
5	$-x^2(1 - x) -2x(x - x^2)$	$x^3 - 3x^2$ $-3x^3 - 3x^2$ $-x^3 - 3x$ $3x^3 - 3x^2$	**6**	$-x(1 - x) - 1 - (x - 1)$	$-x^2 - 2$ $x^2 - 2$ $-x^2 - 2x$ $x^2 - 2x$

Expand and simplify the following.

7 $-10(3 - 2x) =$ ____________

8 $5x(8x - 7) =$ ____________

9 $-(6 - c) =$ ____________

10 $-4a(2x + 4) =$ ____________

11 $2a^3(a + 3b - 7) =$ ____________

12 $3y(x - y + 5z) =$ ____________

13 $2x^2(6x - 1) =$ ____________

14 $-3x(4x - 2x^4) =$ ____________

15 $-2(y + z - 2) + 5y =$ ____________

____

16 $3a(b - 2) - (4 - a) =$ ____________

____

17 $-3x(x - 2) + 2(6x - 5) =$ ____________

____

18 $10a - a^2(a - 5) =$ ____________

____

19 $-7x(1 - x^2) - (10x - 7) + x^2 =$

____

____

20 $-2(a + a^2) - 6a^2(5 - 3a^2) =$

____

____

 ISBN: 9780170447096

Factorising

- Factors are terms that are **multiplied** together (rather than added or subtracted), e.g. 2 and 3 are factors of 6 because 2 **x** 3 = 6.
- In algebra, factorising is the '**undoing**' **of expanding**.
- Expressions with brackets are usually in **factorised form**.

Examples:

Expand →

Factorised form	Unfactorised (expanded) form
$2x(x + 4)$	$2x^2 + 8x$
$-(x - 9)$	$-x + 9$ or $9 - x$
$-3xy^3(2 - y + 5x)$	$-6xy^3 + 3xy^4 - 15x^2y^3$

← Factorise

Remember, if there is **no sign** between a term and a bracket, it is understood that you should **multiply**.

Finding the biggest factor:

- When factorising, you must factorise **completely**. There must be **no common factor** for the terms inside the brackets.
- You need to ask yourself: '**What is the biggest term (highest common factor or HCF) that will divide into every term?**'
- Do not use fractions or decimals when factorising.

Examples:

Terms	Common factors	Highest common factor (HCF)
6 and 12	1, 2, 3, 6	6
$24p$ and $18p$	1, 2, 3, 6, p, $2p$, $3p$, $6p$	$6p$
$15p^2q$ and $6pq^2$	1, 3, p, q, $3p$, $3q$, pq, $3pq$	$3pq$

A Find the common factors of these terms, if any, then highlight the highest.

1 5, 11 ____________________

2 $21x$, $14x$ ____________________

3 $5xy$, $20x$ ____________________

4 $3x^2$, $12x^3$ ____________________

5 $16xy$, $24y^3$ ____________________

____

6 xyz^2, xy^2z, x^2yz ____________________

____

ISBN: 9780170447096

Hints: 1 If you are asked to factorise, check your answer by expanding.
2 If you are asked to expand, check your answer by factorising.

B Fill the boxes with letters and/or numbers in order to complete a correct factorisation.

1 $8xy - 2y = 2y(\square x - 1)$

2 $12x^2 + 9x = 3x(4x + \square)$

3 $35x + 14y = 7(\square x + 2y)$

4 $4x - 20x^2 = 4x(1 - \square)$

5 $x^2y - 2x = x(\square - 2)$

6 $36x + 24 = 12(\square + 2)$

7 $-16x + 20x^2 = -4x(\square - 5x)$

8 $-8xy - 16y = -8y(\square + 2)$

9 $x^2y^2 - 3x + x^2 = x(\square - 3 + x)$

10 $6xyz^2 + 18x^2z = 6xz(\square + \square)$

C Fill the boxes with letters and/or numbers in order to complete a correct factorisation.

1 $5xy + 20y = \square(x + 4)$

2 $9y - 3x = \square(3y - x)$

3 $7x^2 - 21xy = \square(x - 3y)$

4 $15x + 30 - 10y = \square(3x + 6 - 2y)$

5 $12x^2 - 16x = \square(3x - 4)$

6 $18xyz - 6z = \square(3xy - 1)$

7 $24x^3 + 20x^2 = \square(6x + 5)$

8 $-18x - 14 = \square(9x + 7)$

9 $x^2 + 6x - x^3 = \square(x + 6 - x^2)$

10 $15xy^2z - 20yx^2 = \square(3yz - 4x)$

D Write the contents of each bracket in order to complete a correct factorisation.

1 $18xy + 10y = 2y($ ______________ $)$

2 $4x^3 + 12x^2 = 4x^2($ ______________ $)$

3 $15 - 3x + 6y = 3($ ______________ $)$

4 $70x^2 + 14x - 35 = 7($ ______________ $)$

5 $16x + 10 + 24y = 2($ ______________ $)$

6 $44xy - 33y^2 = 11y($ ______________ $)$

7 $2x^2 + 9x - x^3 = x($ ______________ $)$

8 $15x^5 - 9x^2 = 3x^2($ ______________ $)$

9 $-6x - 10 - 2x^4 = -2($ ______________ $)$

10 $-3x^3y^2z + 9xy^3z = -3xy^2z($ ______________ $)$

ISBN: 9780170447096

E Circle/highlight the correct factorised answer for each of the following.

1	$-2x + 8$	$-2(4 - x)$ $-2(x + 4)$ $2(x - 4)$ $2(4 - x)$	**2**	$3x^2 - 12xy$	$3x(x - 4y)$ $-3x(x - 4y)$ $3x(4y - x)$ $-3x(4y - x)$
3	$10x^2 - 20x - 8$	$2(10x - 5x^2 - 4)$ $2(5x^2 - 10x - 4)$ $-2(5x^2 - 10x - 4)$ $-2(4 + 10x - 5x^2)$	**4**	$ab^2c - ba^2c + cab$	$abc(1 + a - b)$ $-abc(a - 1 - b)$ $abc(1 - a + b)$ $-abc(1 + a - b)$

F Factorise the following.

1 $18x - 24x^2 =$ __________

2 $10xy + 6xyz =$ __________

3 $12x^5 + 6x - 15x^2 =$ __________

4 $4c^3 - 8c + 12 =$ __________

5 $7w^4 + 21w - 14w^2 =$ __________

6 $25p^2q^4 - 35pq^3 =$ __________

7 $15ab^4 + 9a^3 - 12ab =$ __________

8 $30j^5k - 6j^2 + 12jk^9 =$ __________

9 $m^6n^3 + m^3n^5 - 3m^7n^2 =$ __________

10 $6g^2h^5 + 8g^3h - 24h^2 =$ __________

11 $-fg^2h^3 - 6f^5g^2h - 3fh^3 =$ __________

12 $60rs^3t^{10} + 15r^2s^2t - 10rst^3 =$ __________

Find the errors

Some of the following statements are correct and some are incorrect. If the statement is correct, put a tick in the ✓/✗ column. If it is incorrect, put a cross in the ✓/✗ column, and write the correct solution.

Expand, simplify and if possible factorise your answer.

		✓/✗	Correct solution
1	$5d - (4 - d) = 4d - 4$		
2	$-9 - 3de(2e^2 - 7d) - d^2e = 20d^2e - 6de^3 - 9$		
3	$-(7de^2 - 1) = 1 - 7de^2$		
4	$7e(d - 5d^2) - 3(2de - 5e) - e(4 + d^2) = de - 34d^2e + 11e$		
5	$6e^6 + 2e(11d^0e^5 - e^5) = 26e^6$		
6	$4(1 - e) - 3(e - 1) = 7(1 - e)$		

Factorise the following.

		✓/✗	Correct solution
7	$4de - 12de^2 + 6e^2d = -2de(3e - 2)$		
8	$36d^3e^2 - 18d^2e^3 = 6de^2(6d^2 - 3de)$		
9	$d^5e^3 - d^2e^4 - d^4e^3f + d^6e^8 = d^2e^3(d^3 - e - d^2f + d^3e^5)$		
10	$-1 - 13d + e = -1(13d + 1 - e)$		

 ISBN: 9780170447096

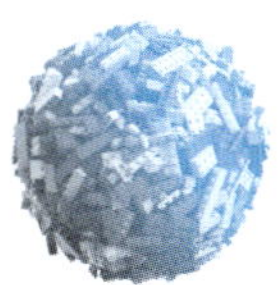

Challenge 3

Highlight the boxes which contain an expression that is equivalent to the central expression.

1

$3(4a-2)+6(1-a)$	$\dfrac{2a^6}{12a^5}$	$5a-(-a)$	$3(4a+2)-6(1-a)$
$48a^3 \div 8a^2$	**$6a$**		$12(a^3)^2 \div 2a^4$
$a + a \times 5$			$5a + (-a)$
$a + a \times 3$	$6(a^3)^2 \div a^5$	$\dfrac{6a^8}{a^7}$	$\dfrac{24a^{10}b}{4a^9b}$

2

$2a^2(9b-3b)$	$\dfrac{36a^6b^6}{3a^3b^6}$	$2a \times 6ab$	$3ab(6a-2)$
$6b \times 2a^2$	**$12a^2b$**		$\dfrac{48a^3b^3}{4ab^2}$
$6b - 4b \times 3a^2$			$8ba^2 + 4a^2b$
$12a^2b^2 - b$	$24a^2b^2 \div 2b$	$3b(2a)^2$	$8ab + 4a$

ISBN: 9780170447096

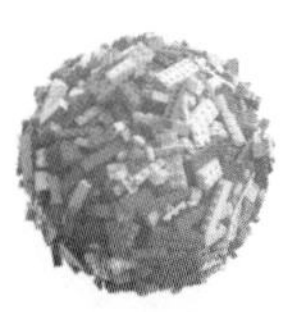

Formulae and substitution

Examples:
This is a cuboid (a box) with sides L, H and D cm long:

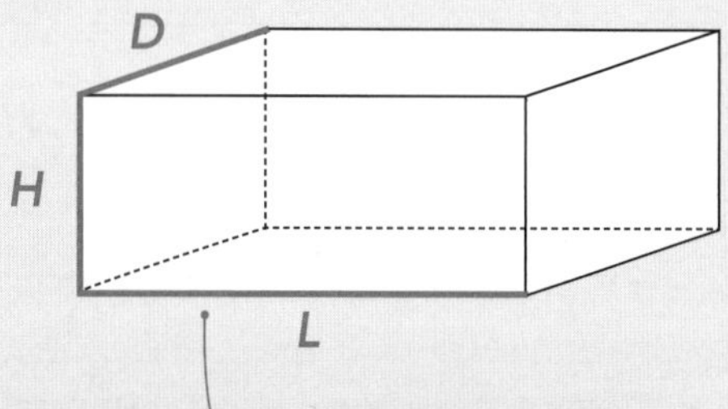

L, ***H*** and ***D*** stand for the **Length**, **Height** and **Depth** of the cuboid, so these are the **variables**.

Surface Area = $2LH + 2LD + 2HD$

$$SA = 2(LH + LD + HD)$$

This is the **formula** for finding the surface area of a cuboid.

Volume = $L \times H \times D$

$$V = LHD$$

This is the **formula** for finding the volume of a cuboid.

Examples:

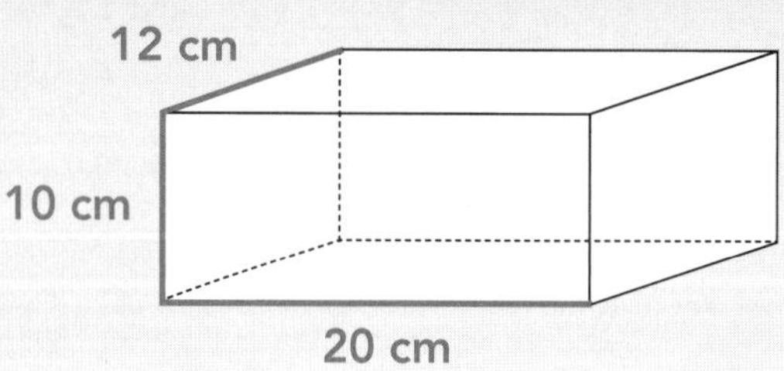

Surface Area: $SA = 2(\mathbf{LH} + \mathbf{LD} + \mathbf{HD})$

$= 2(\mathbf{20 \times 10 + 20 \times 12 + 10 \times 12})$

$= 2(200 + 240 + 120)$

$= 1120\text{ cm}^2$

For this cuboid, we know that $L = 20$, $H = 10$ and $D = 12$.

Volume: $V = \mathbf{LHD}$

$= \mathbf{20 \times 10 \times 12}$

$= 2400\text{ cm}^3$

Don't forget the units.

 ISBN: 9780170447096

1 **a** Use the formulae on the opposite page to calculate the surface area and volume of a box that is 0.9 m long, 0.3 m high and 0.5 m deep.

SA = ______________________ V = ______________________

= ______________________ = ______________________

= ______________________ = ______________________

b Use the formulae on the opposite page to calculate the surface area and volume of a cube with edges 20 cm long.

SA = ______________________ V = ______________________

= ______________________ = ______________________

= ______________________ = ______________________

2 The formula for calculating the area of a trapezium is the average length of the parallel sides (a and b) multiplied by the vertical height:

$$A = \frac{a + b}{2} \times h$$

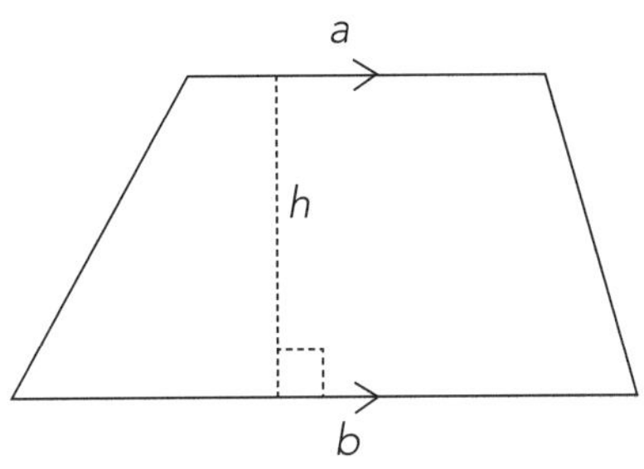

Calculate the areas of the following trapezia.

a

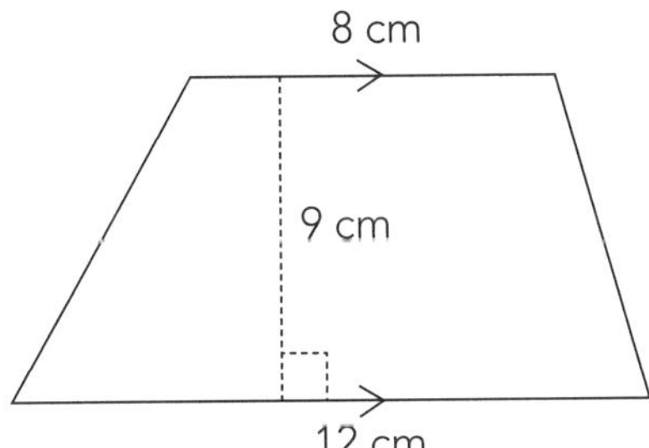

A = ______________________

= ______________________

= ______________________

b

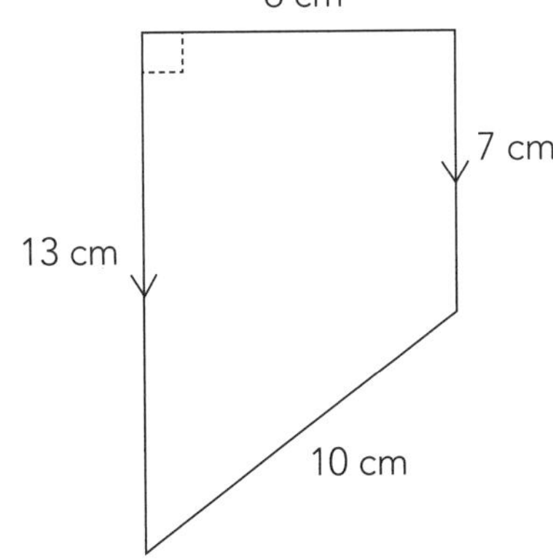

A = ______________________

= ______________________

= ______________________

ISBN: 9780170447096

3 Complete the following table.

Formula	$b = 2, c = -3$	$b = -1, c = 4$	$b = -4, c = -2$
$A = 4b + 3c$	$A =$ ______ $=$ ______ $=$ ______	$A =$ ______ $=$ ______ $=$ ______	$A =$ ______ $=$ ______ $=$ ______
$A = 7 - 5bc$	$A =$ ______ $=$ ______ $=$ ______	$A =$ ______ $=$ ______ $=$ ______	$A =$ ______ $=$ ______ $=$ ______
$A = -b(c - 4)$	$A =$ ______ $=$ ______ $=$ ______	$A =$ ______ $=$ ______ $=$ ______	$A =$ ______ $=$ ______ $=$ ______
$A = c + (b - c)^2$	$A =$ ______ $=$ ______ $=$ ______	$A =$ ______ $=$ ______ $=$ ______	$A =$ ______ $=$ ______ $=$ ______
$A = 2b^2 - 5(c - 2)$	$A =$ ______ $=$ ______ $=$ ______	$A =$ ______ $=$ ______ $=$ ______	$A =$ ______ $=$ ______ $=$ ______
$A = \frac{5b + c^2}{2}$	$A =$ ______ $=$ ______ $=$ ______	$A =$ ______ $=$ ______ $=$ ______	$A =$ ______ $=$ ______ $=$ ______

ISBN: 9780170447096

An investigation

The formula for calculating the amount of energy that a moving body has is $E = \frac{1}{2}mv^2$, where:

E represents **energy** in joules (one joule is approximately the energy you need to pick up an apple)
m represents the **mass** of the object in kilograms
v represents the **velocity** of an object in metres per second.

A small car weighs approximately one tonne, or 1000 kg.

The table below will help you to approximately convert velocity in km/h to velocity in m/s.

km/h	11	22	33	44
m/s	3	6	9	12

Using the formula, we can calculate the amount of energy released when a small car, travelling at a given speed, hits a stationary object (e.g. a tree).

For example: At 11 km/h:

$$E = \frac{1}{2}mv^2$$
$$= \frac{1}{2} \times 1000 \times 3^2$$
$$= 4500 \text{ joules}$$

From the table above, 11 km/h is approximately 3 m/s.

Use the space below to do some similar calculations and complete the table on the next page.

ISBN: 9780170447096

km/h	11	22	33	44
m/s	3	6	9	12
energy (j)	4500			

Use your completed table to help you select the best answer.

1 The energy released when a car travelling at 22 km/h hits a stationary object is

a the same as the energy released by a car travelling at 11 km/h hitting a stationary object. ☐

b double the energy released by a car travelling at 11 km/h hitting a stationary object. ☐

c triple the energy released by a car travelling at 11 km/h hitting a stationary object. ☐

d four times the energy released by a car travelling at 11 km/h hitting a stationary object. ☐

So multiplying the velocity by ____ means the energy released is multiplied by ____.

Complete the following.

2 The energy released when a car travelling at 33 km/h hits a stationary object is

________ times the energy released by a car travelling at 11 km/h.

So multiplying the velocity by ____ means the energy released is multiplied by ____.

3 The energy released when a car travelling at 44 km/h hits a stationary object is

________ times the energy released by a car travelling at 11 km/h.

So multiplying the velocity by ____ means the energy released is multiplied by ____.

4 Complete the table.

If the **velocity** is multiplied by	then the **energy** is multiplied by
2	4
3	
4	
a	

This happens because of the $\mathbf{v}^2$ in $E = \frac{1}{2}m\mathbf{v}^2$

What does this mean? The faster you go, the bigger the mess!

 ISBN: 9780170447096

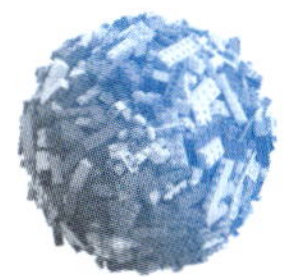

Challenge 4

Some of the following statements are correct and some are incorrect. If the statement is correct, put a tick in the ✓/✗ column. If it is incorrect, put a cross in the ✓/✗ column, and write the correct solution. Substitute with the following values:

$a = -2$ $b = -3$ $c = 5$ $d = -4$ $e = 10$

Hint: Don't forget to use **BEDMAS**.

		✓/✗	Correct solution
1	$a(c - b^2) = (-2) \times (5 - (-3)^2)$ $= 8$		
2	$\frac{a^2c}{-e} = \frac{(-2)^2 \times 5}{-10}$ $= 2$		
3	$-e\left(\frac{e-d}{a}\right) = -10\left(\frac{10-(-4)}{-2}\right)$ $= -70$		
4	$(b - c)^2 + ae = ((-3) - 5)^2 + (-2) \times 10$ $= 84$		
5	$\sqrt{c^2(-d)} = \sqrt{5^2 \times (-(-4))}$ $= 10$		
6	$ab - \frac{-a^2}{e} = ((-2) \times (-3)) - \frac{-(-2)^2}{10}$ $= 6.4$		
7	$\frac{abd}{-e^2} = \frac{(-2) \times (-3) \times (-4)}{(-10)^2}$ $= -0.24$		
8	$ade - \frac{d^2}{a} = ((-2) \times (-4) \times 10) - \frac{(-4)^2}{-2}$ $= 88$		
9	$\frac{bd}{-a} - \frac{\sqrt{a^2}}{d} = \frac{(-3) \times (-4)}{-(-2)} - \frac{\sqrt{(-2)^2}}{-4}$ $= 5.5$		

ISBN: 9780170447096

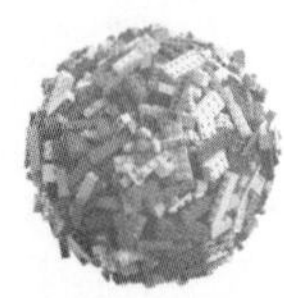

Solving linear equations

- 'Solve' means '**find the value for x**'.

Rules: 1 You can do anything you like to an equation as long as you do the **same to both sides**.

2 There should be only **one equals sign** per line.

3 Collect all the variables on one side and numbers on the other side.

4 When you want to get rid of something, perform the **opposite** operation.

5 Your aim is to get **x = ...**

Two-step equations

- First collect all the terms with variables (e.g. x) on the left, and all the numbers on the right.
- Do the adding or subtracting **before** the multiplying or dividing.

Examples:

1

$$5x - 3.5 = 12$$

$$5x - 3.5 + 3.5 = 12 + 3.5$$

First adding/subtracting: **add 3.5** to both sides.

$$5x = 15.5$$

$$\frac{5x}{5} = \frac{15.5}{5}$$

Then multiplying/dividing: **divide** both sides by **5**.

$$x = 3.1$$

An extra trick:

Sometimes the **variable** is on the **right**-hand side. Example: $22 = 2 - 8x$.

Because both sides are equal to each other, you can **flip** them around:

$$22 = 2 - 8x \quad \text{so} \quad 2 - 8x = 22$$

2

$$22 = 2 - 8x$$

$$2 - 8x = 22$$

$$2 - 8x - 2 = 22 - 2$$

First adding/subtracting: **subtract 2** from both sides.

$$-8x = 20$$

$$\frac{-8x}{-8} = \frac{20}{-8}$$

Then multiplying/dividing: **divide** both sides by **−8**.

$$x = -2.5$$

 ISBN: 9780170447096

Solve the following.

1 $7x + 24 = 3$

2 $28 = 3a - 5$

3 $2y + 13 = 6$

4 $5z + 8 = -7$

5 $5p - 1 = 1.5$

6 $12d + 9 = 6$

7 $-32 = 6k - 8$

8 $11 = 7x + 60$

9 $10 = 4t - 12$

10 $24 - 21 - 3g$

11 $0 = 5a + 25$

12 $10 = 1 - 3x$

ISBN: 9780170447096

Write an equation for each of the following, and then solve it to find the mystery number. Use the variable x to represent the number.

13 If a number is tripled, and then seven is subtracted, the answer is thirty-eight.

14 A number is doubled, and then eleven is added. The answer is twenty.

15 When three is subtracted from eight times a number, the answer is nine.

16 If 5.4 is added to seven times a number, the answer is four.

Write equations for the following situations, using the variables in brackets. Then solve the equation in order to answer the question.

17 Suzie is one year younger than triple Pene's age (p). Suzie is fourteen. How old is Pene?

18 Bus fares to and from work cost Hemi \$4 per day. On Monday he worked for six hours, and took home \$71. How much is he paid (p) per hour?

19 Mila is paid \$3 per hour plus \$$x$ per punnet for picking strawberries. On Wednesday she worked for five hours and picked 80 punnets. She earned \$63. How much is she paid for each punnet?

20 When Mila picks raspberries she is paid \$3 per hour (h) plus \$1.20 per punnet. On Thursday she picked 50 punnets of raspberries, and was paid \$73.50. How long did she work for?

 ISBN: 9780170447096

For each of the following diagrams, write an equation using x as the variable. Then solve it in order to answer the question.

21 Each edge of a cube is $x + 0.5$ cm long. If the total length of all the edges is 24 cm, calculate the value of x.

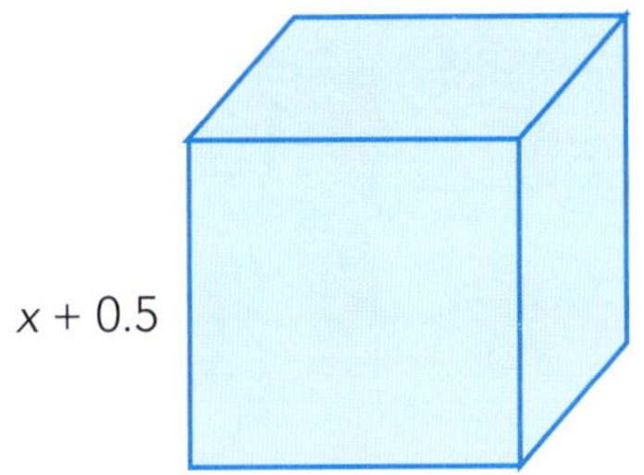

22 The total length of all the edges of this cuboid is 46 cm. Calculate the value of x, and use it to write down the dimensions of the cuboid.

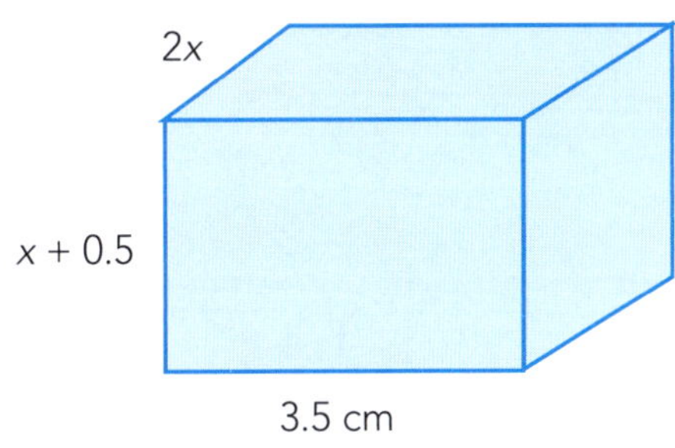

23 Calculate the value of x, and use it to calculate the sizes of the angles in this triangle.

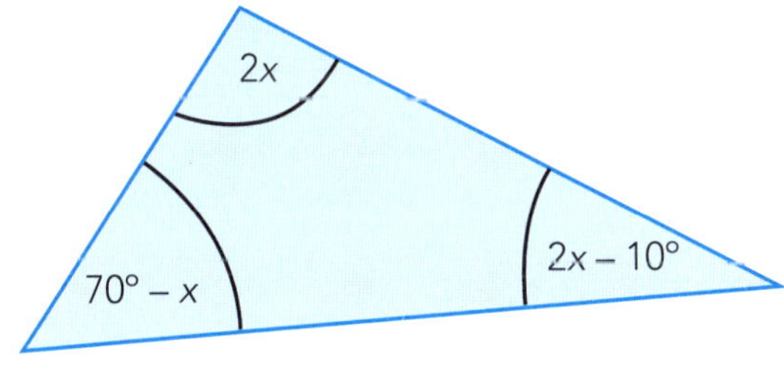

24 Calculate the value of x, and use it to calculate the sizes of the angles in this triangle.

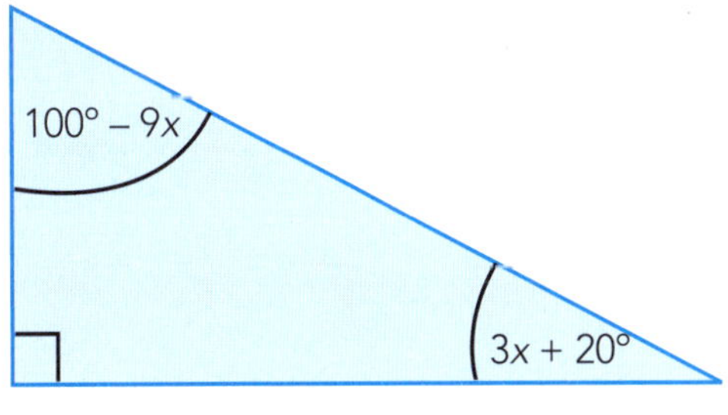

ISBN: 9780170447096

Equations with fractions

- First add or subtract so that the fraction is on its own on one side of the equation.
- Then multiply both sides by the denominator.

Examples:

1

$$\frac{2b-3}{7} = 9$$

The fraction is already on its own, so **multiply** both sides by $\frac{7}{1}$.

$$\frac{7}{1} \times \frac{2b-3}{7} = 9 \times \frac{7}{1}$$

$$2b - 3 = 63$$

$$2b - 3 + 3 = 63 + 3$$

Add 3 to both sides.

$$2b = 66$$

$$b = 33$$

2

$$5 - \frac{3c}{4} = 8$$

The fraction is not on its own, so **subtract 5** from both sides.

$$5 - \frac{3c}{4} - 5 = 8 - 5$$

$$-\frac{3c}{4} = 3$$

The fraction is already on its own, so **multiply** both sides by $\frac{4}{1}$.

$$\frac{4}{1} \times -\frac{3c}{4} = 3 \times \frac{4}{1}$$

$$-3c = 12$$

Divide both sides by **–3**.

$$c = -4$$

Solve the following.

1 $\frac{k}{7} + 9 = 16$

2 $\frac{5x+2}{4} = 8$

 ISBN: 9780170447096

3 $2 + \frac{x}{3} = 6$

4 $\frac{3 - x}{2} = 5$

5 $\frac{11 - 2x}{3} = 7$

6 $9 - \frac{7x}{6} = 2$

7 $1 = 3 + \frac{x}{9}$

8 $1 + \frac{3x + 2}{2} = 5$

9 $15 - \frac{17x + 18}{3} = 9$

10 $11 + \frac{4x}{5} = 9$

11 $15 - \frac{8x}{3} = 11$

12 $5 - \frac{15x + 2}{4} = 12$

ISBN: 9780170447096

Write an equation for each of the following, and then solve it to find the mystery number. Use the variable x to represent the number.

13 A number is halved, and then seven is subtracted from it. The answer is five.

14 Five is added to double a number, and the result is divided by three. The answer is seven.

15 The difference between triple a number and ten is halved. The answer is four.

16 A fifth of the sum of triple a number and seven has two subtracted from it. The answer is three.

Write equations for the following situations, using the variables indicated. Then solve the equation in order to answer the question.

17 Ria, Carter and Tama are working for their dad collecting cones. He paid them $\$b$ for every bag of cones, plus \$12 for stacking the bags in the shed. They filled and stacked twenty bags. If they shared the money equally, and earned \$34 each, calculate how much Dad paid for each bag of cones.

18 Ria, Carter and Tama's aunty manages motels. She pays them \$25 for cleaning a motel, plus \$4 for each bed that they make. On Saturday they worked together to clean five motels and they made some beds (b). If they shared their earnings equally, and each earned \$59, how many beds did they make?

 ISBN: 9780170447096

Equations with variables on both sides

- Remember, **first** add and/or subtract to collect all the terms with variables (e.g. x) on the left, and all the numbers on the right.
- **Then** do any multiplying or dividing needed.
- Remember: when solving algebra equations, the answers can be positive or negative, and whole numbers or decimals.

Examples:

1

$$7x + 23 = 2 + x$$
$$7x + 23 - x = 2 + x - x$$
$$6x + 23 = 2$$
$$6x + 23 - 23 = 2 - 23$$
$$6x = -21$$
$$\frac{6x}{6} = \frac{21}{6}$$
$$x = -3.5$$

First adding/subtracting: **subtract x** from both sides. Then **subtract 23** from both sides.

Then multiplying/dividing: **divide** both sides by **6**.

2

$$5 + 2x = 4x + 1$$
$$5 + 2x - 4x = 4x + 1 - 4x$$
$$5 - 2x = 1$$
$$5 - 2x - 5 = 1 - 5$$
$$-2x = -4$$
$$\frac{-2x}{-2} = \frac{-4}{-2}$$
$$x = 2$$

First adding/subtracting: **subtract 4x** from both sides. Then **subtract 5** from both sides.

Notice that now we have just an x term on the left and a constant on the right.

Then multiplying/dividing: **divide** both sides by **−2**.

A trick for example 2: $5 + 2x = 4x + 1$

The right side has more x's than the left.

Because both sides must be equal to each other, you can **flip** them around:

$(5 + 2x) = (4x + 1)$ so $4x + 1 = 5 + 2x$

If you do this, the coefficient of x will be positive, so you will not need to divide by a negative number.

Solve the following.

1 $1 - 4x = 15 + 3x$

2 $6y + 9 = 2y - 11$

3 $100 + 2b = 15 - 8b$

4 $13a + 2 = a - 28$

5 $7x + 9 = 2x - 6$

6 $1 + 8c + 7 = 3c - 4$

Hint: For numbers **7** to **10**, use the trick on page 43.

7 $3 + 7p = 27p + 17$

8 $15 + 7f = 9f - 2$

9 $30 - x = 4 + 12x$

10 $4 + 2x = 7x + 9$

ISBN: 9780170447096

Write an equation for each of the following, and then solve it to find the mystery number. Use the variable x to represent the number.

11 Multiplying a number by four and then adding seven gives the same answer as subtracting fourteen from it.

12 Subtracting a number from thirteen gives the same answer as subtracting five from twice the number.

13 Dividing a number by three gives the same answer as five less than double the number.

14 Half a number is the same as fourteen reduced by triple the number.

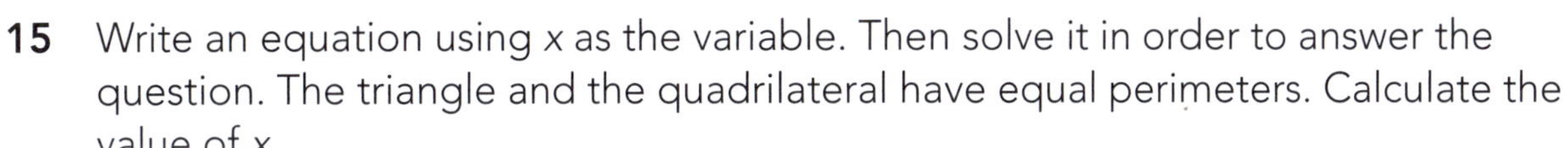

15 Write an equation using x as the variable. Then solve it in order to answer the question. The triangle and the quadrilateral have equal perimeters. Calculate the value of x.

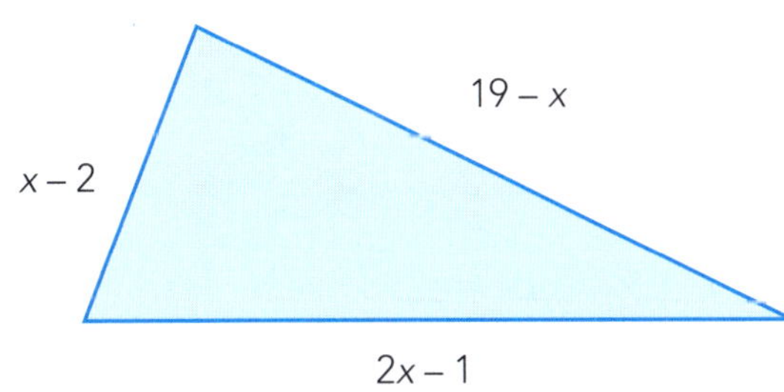

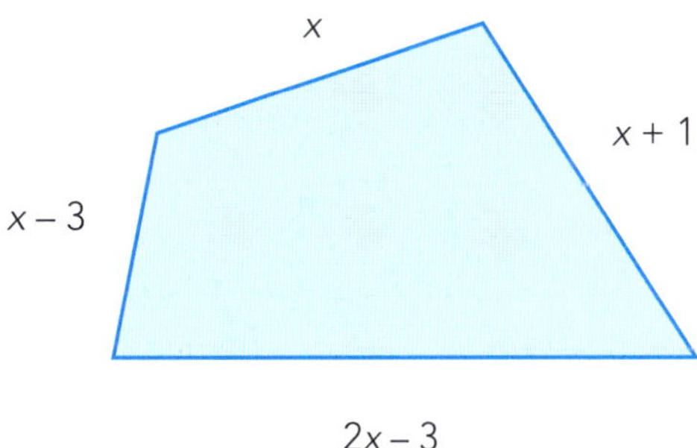

ISBN: 9780170447096

Equations with brackets

- Expand the brackets first, before solving the same way as you did in the last exercise.

The order of operations for solving an equation:

1. Multiply to get rid of fractions
2. Expand the brackets
3. Add/subtract like terms
4. Multiply/divide.

Examples:

1

$$\frac{5(2p-1)}{7} = p - 11$$

$$\frac{5(2p-1)}{7} \times \frac{7}{1} = p \times \frac{7}{1} - 11 \times \frac{7}{1}$$

1 Multiply every term by $\frac{7}{1}$ to get rid of fractions.

$$5(2p-1) = 7p - 77$$

$$10p - 5 = 7p - 77$$

2 Expand the brackets.

$$3p = -72$$

3 Add 5 to both sides. Subtract $7p$ from both sides.

$$p = -24$$

4 Divide both sides by 3.

2

$$\frac{2m}{3} - 1 = 4(m-2)$$

$$\frac{2m}{3} \times \frac{3}{1} - 1 \times \frac{3}{1} = \frac{3}{1} \times 4(m-2)$$

1 Multiply every term by $\frac{3}{1}$ to get rid of fractions.

$$2m - 3 = 12(m-2)$$

$$2m - 3 = 12m - 24$$

2 Expand the brackets.

$$12m - 24 = 2m - 3$$

Flip the sides so the $12m$ is on the left.

$$10m = 21$$

3 Subtract $2m$ from both sides. Add 24 to both sides.

$$m = 2.1$$

4 Divide both sides by 10.

ISBN: 9780170447096

Puzzle

Below is a correctly assembled jigsaw puzzle. Note that each piece fits with another by having equivalent expressions on each edge.

- Study the puzzle to make sure that you understand how it works.
- Take a photograph of it in case you get stuck reassembling it.
- Cut the pieces up and then mix them up.
- Match edges with equivalent expressions in order to reassemble it.

$(4b^5)^0$ $2b^2 - b - 2b^2 + 3b$	1 $\frac{2a^5b^6}{6b^4a^5}$ $b^2 \times b^3 \times b^4$	$\frac{b^2}{3}$ $4b^2 + 2b^5 - 6b^3$ $-3b(b - 4)$	$2b^2(2 + b^3 - 3b)$ $9b^3 \div 3b^5$
$2b$ $-2b < 8$ $\frac{b}{5} + 2 = 4$	b^9 $b > -4$ $2^b = 16$ $b + b$	$-3b^2 + 12b$ $b = 4$ $4b + 16 = 0$ $2 - (10 - b) = 13$	$\frac{3}{b^2}$ $b = -4$ $b \times b$
$b = 10$ $b(b - 4) = 0$ $\frac{(2b^2)^5}{2(4b^4)^2}$	$2b$ $b = 0$ or $b = 4$ $b^2 - 16 = 0$ $(4b^4e)^2 \div 2(2b^3e)$	$b = 21$ $b = \pm 4$ $8b - 2 = 9b + 2$ $5.5 = \frac{b - 11}{2}$	b^2 $b = -4$ $a^3b^4 \times a^3b \div (a^2b)^3$
b^2 $b^3 = 64$ $\frac{8b^5c^6}{4b^4c^6}$	$4b^5e$ $b = 4$ $4b - 16 = 0$ $-b^2 + 2b^2 - 2b^2 + 2b^2$	$b = 22$ $b = 4$ $(b - 4)(b + 4) = 0$ $\frac{2b}{4} > b + 2$	b^2 $b = \pm 4$ $-4b - b^2 + b^2 + 6b$
$2b$ $b^2 + 8x + 16 = 0$	b^2 $b = -4$ $b(b + 4) = 0$	$b < -4$ $b = -4$ or $b = 0$ $4b^2 - 64 = 0$	$2b$ $b = \pm 4$

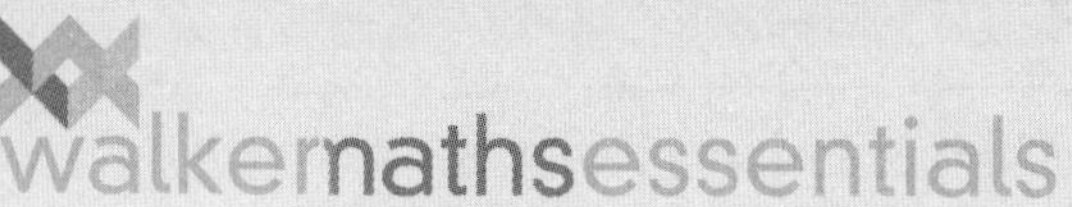

Mix and match

Each of the columns below contain a dark blue instruction header, matching examples of questions (pale blue) and the corresponding answers (white).

- Study the chart to make sure that you understand how it works.
- Take a photograph of it in case you get stuck reassembling it.
- Match five pale blue question boxes to each dark blue instruction header.
- Then match a white answer box to each pale blue question box.

Solve	Evaluate	Expand	Simplify	Factorise
$12x - 8 = 70$	If $x = 2$ and $y = 9$ $\frac{y - x}{x}$	$-2x(x - 4)$	$6x^2 - y - 5x^2 + y$	$28x - 16x^2$
$x = 6.5$	3.5	$8x - 2x^2$	x^2	$4x(7 - 4x)$
$-5 + \frac{x}{4} = -19$	If $x = -1$ and $y = -3$ $2(x^2 + 4y)$	$3x(-x - 4)$	$\frac{-28x^6y^2}{-14x^4y^2}$	$-12x^3y - 6x^2y$
$x = 56$	-22	$-3x^2 - 12x$	$2x^2$	$-6x^2y(2x + 1)$
$6 + 2x = 3x - 1$	If $x = 2$ and $y = -3$ $xy - 3x^2$	$(x + 2)(x - 1)$	$(3x^3y^0)^3$	$x^2 - 5x + 6$
$x = 7$	-18	$x^2 + x - 2$	$27x^9$	$(x - 3)(x - 2)$
$-2(x + 4) = -12$	If $x = 0$ and $y = 2$ $6^x - y$	$(x - 2)^2$	$x^6y^7 \div x^3y^6$	$x^2 - 49$
$x = 2$	-1	$x^2 - 4x + 4$	x^3y	$(x - 7)(x + 7)$
A number is halved then eight is subtracted from it. The answer is six.	If $x = -3$ and $y = -1$ $x^2 - 2y$	$2(x^2 - 2x + 2)$	$2x^2 - x^2 + 3x^2 - x^2$	$3x^2 - 12x + 9$
$x = 28$	11	$2x^2 - 4x + 4$	$3x^2$	$3(x - 3)(x - 1)$

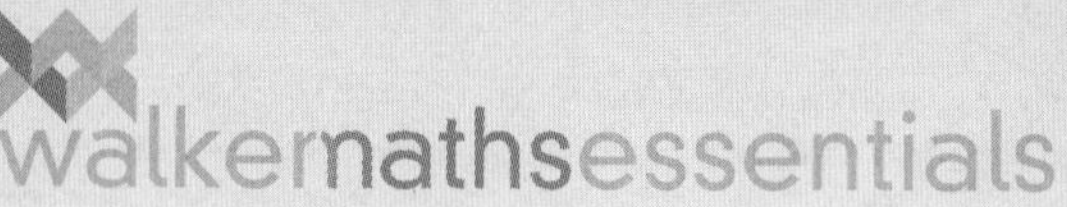
walkermathsessentials

Solve the following.

1 $3(4x + 7) = -9$

2 $10(4 - x) = -2x$

3 $-(6x + 17) = 11 + 2x$

4 $2 - (10 - 3x) = x - 15$

5 $7(5 - 2x) = 4(6 - x) - 13$

6 $17 - 6(4 - 2x) = 2(9x - 5)$

7 $\frac{13x}{2} = 5(x - 3)$

8 $9 = \frac{5(x + 7)}{4}$

9 $\frac{2(4 - 5x)}{7} = 4$

10 $4(5 + x) = \frac{2x}{3}$

Hints: For numbers 11 to 14: 1 Use the swapping sides trick.
2 Don't forget to multiply every term by the denominator.

11 $1 + \frac{15x}{2} = 4(2x - 7)$

12 $\frac{7x}{3} - 2 = 4(2 + x)$

13 $\frac{2(x - 2)}{3} - 7 = 9x$

14 $\frac{3(2 - 7x)}{5} = -(2 + x)$

15 The total length of the edges of the square-based pyramid is the same as that of the cube. Each edge of the pyramid is x cm long, and each edge of the cube is $(x - 3)$ cm long. Calculate their dimensions.

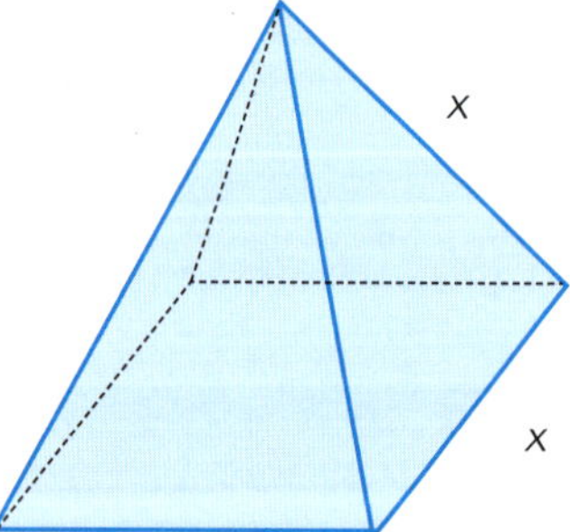

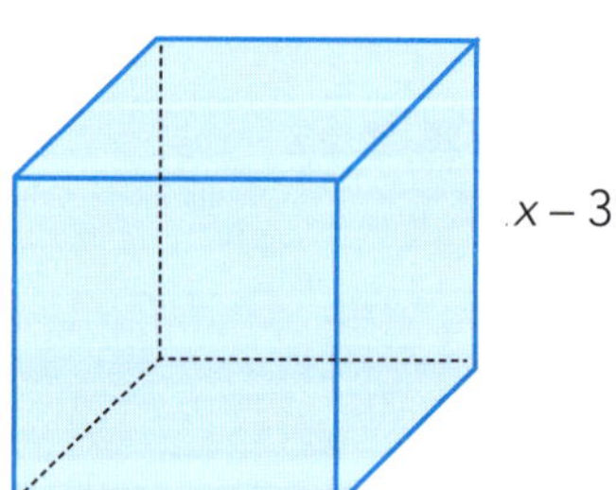

 ISBN: 9780170447096

Inequations

- Inequations have <, >, ≤ or ≥ signs:
  - $<$ means 'is less than'
  - $>$ means 'is greater than'
  - $\leq$ means 'is less than or equal to', 'is at most'
  - $\geq$ means 'is greater than or equal to', 'is at least'.
- You solve an inequation in **exactly** the same way as you solve an equation **except**:

  if you need to **multiply or divide** the equation by a **negative** number,

  or if you use the **trick** and **flip** the sides,

  then you must **reverse the sign.**

Examples:

1

$7x < 21$ (÷ 7)

$x < \frac{21}{7}$

$x < 3$

2

$5x - 3 \geq 17$ (+ 3)

$5x \geq 20$ (÷ 5)

$x \geq \frac{20}{5}$

$x \geq 4$

3

$9 - 4x \leq 33$ (– 9)

$-4x \leq 24$ (÷ by –4)

$x \geq -6$

Dividing by a **negative** number ⇒ **reverse** the sign.

4

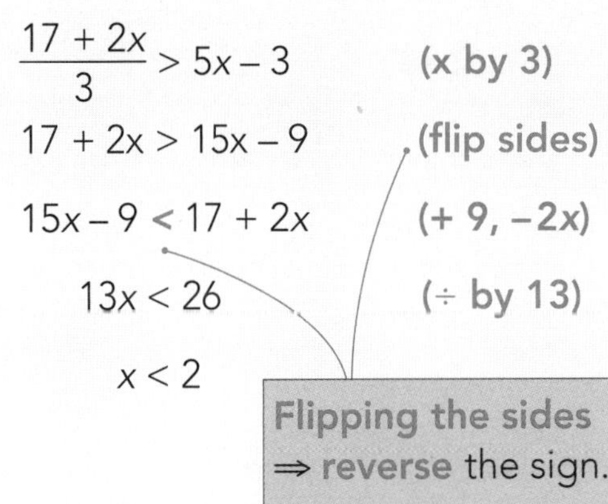

$\frac{17 + 2x}{3} > 5x - 3$ (x by 3)

$17 + 2x > 15x - 9$ (flip sides)

$15x - 9 < 17 + 2x$ (+ 9, –2x)

$13x < 26$ (÷ by 13)

$x < 2$

Flipping the sides ⇒ **reverse** the sign.

Solve the following.

1 $9x > 18$

____

____

____

2 $2x - 11 < 7$

____

____

____

ISBN: 9780170447096

3 $3(x + 4) \geq 0$

4 $17x + 20 \leq x - 12$

5 $5 - x < 7$

6 $3x - 10 \geq 2 + 7x$

7 $11 - x > 2x - 7$

8 $x - 19 < 11x + 5$

9 $x > \frac{x}{4} - 6$

10 $\frac{x}{3} > x + 4$

11 $\frac{7x}{5} < 3x + 8$

12 $\frac{3x - 8}{2} \geq 4x + 1$

 ISBN: 9780170447096

Write an inequation for each of the following situations, and then solve it in order to answer the question.

13 Annie needs to save at least \$156 to pay for a sports trip. She earns \$12 per hour working in a plant nursery. Calculate the minimum number of hours she needs to work in order to earn enough.

14 When a helicopter company transports passengers into a remote area, the weight of each passenger plus their luggage can be up to 80 kg. The company charges extra for any additional weight. Moana weighs 59 kg. Calculate the maximum her luggage can weigh without her paying extra.

15 The sum of the length, width and height of cabin baggage on Air New Zealand has to be less than 118 cm. Emily's bag is 65 cm long and 29 cm deep. Calculate the maximum width her bag can be if it is to be allowed in the cabin.

16 Frank has earned \$88. He owes his mum \$23, and he needs to buy birthday presents (the same) for his twin brothers. If he repays his mum, calculate the maximum amount he can spend on each twin.

17 A truck is allowed to carry up to 1 tonne (1000 kg). It has to carry a 50 kg bag of fertiliser and as many concrete pavers as possible. Each paver weighs 9 kg. Calculate the maximum number of pavers the truck is allowed to carry.

18 The school drama performance needs to raise more than \$400. The board of trustees is giving them \$50. Tickets will sell for \$4 each. Calculate the minimum number of tickets they will need to sell in order to raise more than \$400.

ISBN: 9780170447096

Find the errors

Some of the following equations are solved correctly and some aren't. If the equation is solved correctly, put a tick in the ✓/✗ column. If not, put a cross in the ✓/✗ column, highlight the mistake, and write the correct solution.

		✓/✗	Correct solution
1	$\frac{3x-2}{5} - 8 = x + 3$ $3x - 2 - 8 = 5x + 15$ $5x + 15 = 3x - 10$ $2x = -5$ $x = -2.5$		
2	$8(2x - 1) + 3 = 5 - 4(5x + 1)$ $16x - 8 + 3 = 5 - 20x - 4$ $36x = 6$ $x = \frac{1}{6}$		
3	$4(5 - 2x) - 6 \leq 3x - 8$ $20 - 8x - 6 \leq 3x - 8$ $3x - 8 \leq 14 - 8x$ $11x \leq 22$ $x \leq 2$		
4	$5(2x - 3) = \frac{3x + 4}{2}$ $10(4x - 6) = 3x + 4$ $40x - 60 = 3x + 4$ $37x = 64$ $x = \frac{64}{37}$		
5	$5 - (2 - x) > 11 - 3x$ $5 - 2 + x > 11 - 3x$ $4x > 8$ $x > 2$		

ISBN: 9780170447096

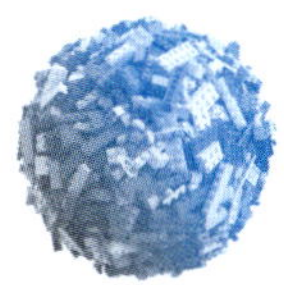

Solving exponential equations

- In exponential equations, the unknown is the exponent (power).
- **Remember:**

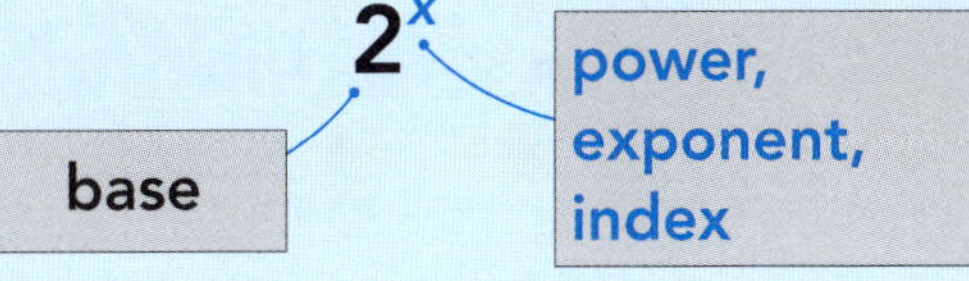

- The only way for you to solve these is by **listing the powers** of the base.
- When graphed, exponential expressions form curves like these:

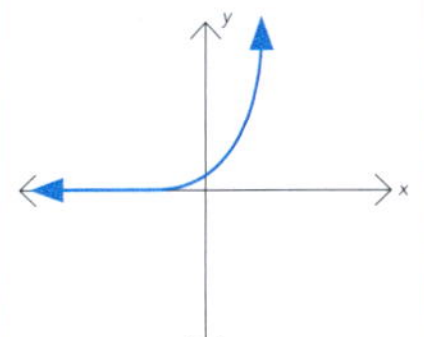

or

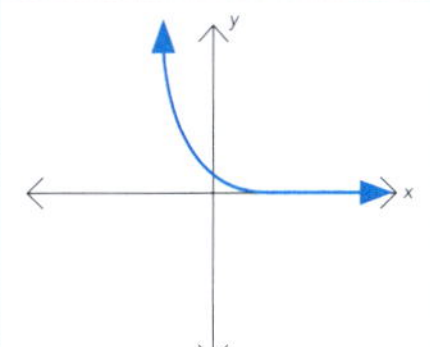

Remember: **anything**^{0} = 1

Examples: 1 $2^x = 32$

List the powers of 2:

$2^0 = 1$
$2^1 = 2$
$2^2 = 4$
$2^3 = 8$
$2^4 = 16$
$\mathbf{2^5 = 32}$

$\therefore\ 2^x = 32 = 2^5$
So $x = 5$

2 $3^x = 81$

List the powers of 3:

$3^0 = 1$
$3^1 = 3$
$3^2 = 9$
$3^3 = 27$
$\mathbf{3^4 = 81}$

$\therefore\ 3^x = 81 = 3^4$
So $x = 4$

Solve the following.

1 $2^x = 8$

____

2 $2^x = 64$

3 $3^x = 27$

4 $4^x = 16$

ISBN: 9780170447096

5 $5^x = 125$

6 $4^x = 64$

7 $9^x = 9$

8 $12^x = 1$

9 $7^x + 1 = 50$

10 $\frac{2^x}{4} = 32$

11 $10^x - 150 = 850$

12 $10^x = 1\ 000\ 000$

13 A bacterium splits itself into two bacteria after an hour. Then each of the new bacteria splits into two after the next hour, and so on. The number of bacteria present depends on how many hours have passed.

a Complete the table below.

Number of hours that have passed (*h*)	0	1	2	3	4	5	6	7	h
Number of bacteria (*b*)	1	2	4	8					
***b* expressed as a power of 2**	2^0	2^1	2^2						

b Explain how the table would change if the bacteria split into three every hour.

ISBN: 9780170447096

Mixing it up

Solve the following.

1 $\frac{11x + 15}{2} - 5 = 3x$

2 $9 - 13x = 2x + 54$

3 $17 - x \leq 5x - 13$

4 $3^x - 6 = 75$

5 $2x - 9 = \frac{3(x - 2)}{5} + 2$

6 $5(3x + 7) - (2x - 11) = 2(x + 1)$

7 $\frac{x^5}{8} = 4$

8 $\frac{3x}{5} + 1 = x - 7$

9 $7 - 2x < 3x - 13$

10 $7 + x^7 = 135$

11 $4 - \frac{11 - x}{6} = 15 + 2x$

12 $11(x + 5) = 27 + 2(3x - 1)$

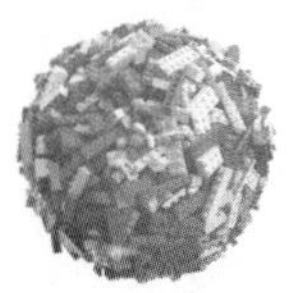

Solving simultaneous equations

- 'Simultaneous' means '**at the same time**'.
- For simultaneous equations you need to be able to solve **two equations** that are **both true 'at the same time'**.
- Because there are two equations, there are also **two variables**.
- There are **two methods** for solving these, and which one you use depends on how the equations are structured.

1 Substitution

- Substitution is easiest where one of the equations is expressed as **$x =$ ……** or **$y =$ …….**
- As the name suggests, you simply substitute the **$x =$ ……** or **$y =$ ……** into the other equation.
- You should number each equation, and say what you are doing at each step.

Examples:

1 Solve the equations $x = 2y$ and $x + y = 12$

$x =$ ….

$x = 2y$ ①

$x + y = 12$ ②

Number each equation.

Substitute ① into ②: $2y + y = 12$

You can write **2y** instead of **x** because they are equal.

$3y = 12$

$\mathbf{y = 4}$

Substitute for y in ①: $x = 2(4)$

$\mathbf{x = 8}$

2 Solve the equations $y + 2x = 10$ and $y = x + 1$

$y =$ ….

$y = x + 1$ ①

$y + 2x = 10$ ②

Substitute ① into ②: $x + 1 + 2x = 10$

You can write **x + 1** instead of **y** because they are equal.

$3x + 1 = 10$

$3x = 9$

$\mathbf{x = 3}$

Substitute for x in ①: $y = 3 + 1$

$\mathbf{y = 4}$

 ISBN: 9780170447096

Solve the following.

1

$$x = 3y$$
$$x + 2y = 20$$

2

$$y = x + 1$$
$$5x + y = 37$$

3

$$5x + y = 45$$
$$y = 4x$$

4

$$x - y = 8$$
$$y = 2 - x$$

5

$$x = 4 + y$$
$$y + 2x = 26$$

6

$$3x + 2y = 13$$
$$y = 5 - 2x$$

7

$$x = 1 + y$$
$$2x - y = 9$$

8

$$x = 3y$$
$$15 + 2x = y$$

ISBN: 9780170447096

Write two equations for each of the following situations, and then solve them simultaneously.

9
- Albert has twice as many lollies as Fred.
- Altogether they have 39 lollies.

How many does each person have?
Let x be the number that Albert has, and y be the number that Fred has.

______
______
______
______
______
______

Albert has ______ lollies, and Fred has ______.

10
- Ana has four more lollies than Max.
- Altogether they have 32 lollies.

How many does each person have?
Let x be the number that Ana has, and y be the number that Max has.

______
______
______
______
______
______

Ana has ______ lollies, and Max has ______.

11
- An adult's ticket to a movie costs three dollars less than double the cost of a child's ticket.
- It cost \$25 for one adult and two children to go to the movie.

Calculate the prices of both types of ticket.
Let y be the price of an adult's ticket, and x be the price of a child's ticket.

______
______
______
______
______
______

An adult's ticket costs \$ ______, and a child's ticket costs \$______.

12
- An adult's ticket to the zoo costs five dollars more than double the cost of a child's ticket.
- It cost \$78 for three adults and one child to go to the zoo.

Calculate the prices of both types of ticket.
Let y be the price of an adult's ticket, and x be the price of a child's ticket.

______
______
______
______
______
______

An adult's ticket costs \$ ______, and a child's ticket costs \$______.

ISBN: 9780170447096

2 Elimination

- Elimination is easiest when the two equations have the same structure.

For example:

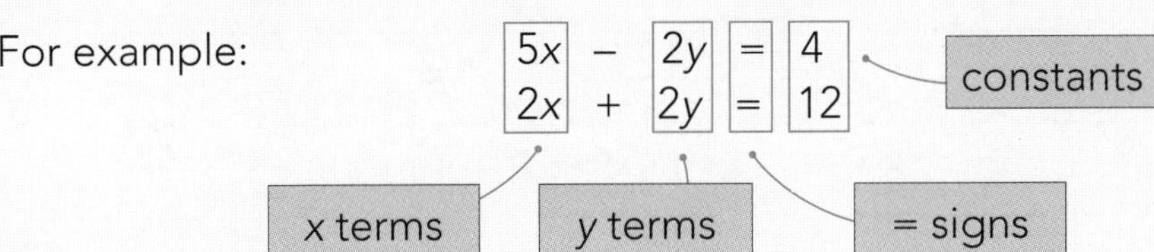

- You solve these by multiplying one or both equations by a constant in order to make either the x terms or the y terms the **same size** but with **different signs**.
- Then **add** the two equations to produce an equation with one variable only.
- You should number each equation, and say what you are doing at each step.

Examples:

1 Solve the equations $5x - 2y = 4$ and $3x + 2y = 12$.

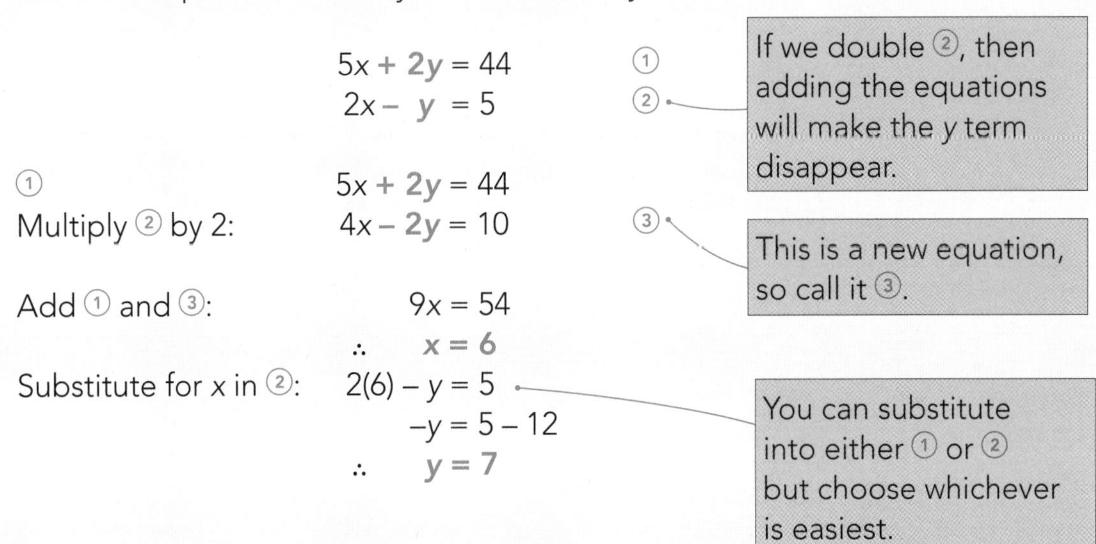

$5x - 2y = 4$ ①
$3x + 2y = 12$ ②

If we add ① and ②, the y terms disappear.

Add ① and ②: $8x = 16$
$\therefore$ $\mathbf{x = 2}$
Substitute for x in ①: $5(2) - 2y = 4$
$\therefore$ $\mathbf{y = 3}$

2 Solve the equations $5x + 2y = 44$ and $2x - y = 5$.

$5x + 2y = 44$ ①
$2x - y = 5$ ②

If we double ②, then adding the equations will make the y term disappear.

① $5x + 2y = 44$
Multiply ② by 2: $4x - 2y = 10$ ③

This is a new equation, so call it ③.

Add ① and ③: $9x = 54$
$\therefore$ $\mathbf{x = 6}$
Substitute for x in ②: $2(6) - y = 5$
$-y = 5 - 12$
$\therefore$ $\mathbf{y = 7}$

You can substitute into either ① or ② but choose whichever is easiest.

ISBN: 9780170447096

Solve the following.

1

$$4x + y = 24$$
$$2x - y = 6$$

2

$$5x + 2y = 14$$
$$3x - 2y = 2$$

Hint: Rearrange **3** and **4** so they have the same structure.

3

$$x - 3y = 7$$
$$3y + 2x = 23$$

4

$$y + 5x = 27$$
$$4x - y = 9$$

5

$$7x + 2y = 20$$
$$3x - y = 3$$

6

$$5x + y = 11$$
$$x - 3y = -1$$

7

$$2x + 5y = 22$$
$$x - y = 4$$

8

$$2y - 3x = 3$$
$$y + x = 14$$

ISBN: 9780170447096

Write two equations for each of the following situations, and then solve them simultaneously.

9
- The sum of the ages of Georgia and her mum is 47.
- The difference between their ages is 19 years.

How old are they?
Let y be Georgia's mum's age, and x be Georgia's age.

____
____
____
____
____
____

Georgia is ______ , and her mum is ______.

10
- The difference between Hemi's dad's age and Hemi's age is 22.
- The sum of Hemi's age and double his dad's age is 83.

How old are they?
Let y be Hemi's dad's age, and x be Hemi's age.

____
____
____
____
____
____

Hemi is ______ , and his dad is ______.

11
- The difference between the price of two muffins and one sandwich is $5.
- A muffin and three sandwiches cost $13.

Calculate the prices of muffins and sandwiches.
Let y be the price of a muffin, and x be the price of a sandwich.

____
____
____
____
____
____

A muffin costs $ ______, and a sandwich costs $______.

12
- Three juicies and two apples cost $6.50.
- The difference between the cost of two juicies and an apple is $2.

Calculate the prices of juicies and apples.
Let y be the price of a juicy, and x be the price of an apple.

____
____
____
____
____
____

A juicy costs $ ______, and an apple costs $______.

Mixing it up

Do the working needed to complete the cross-number in your exercise book.

1		2	3		4	5
			6	7		
8		9		10	11	
					12	13
14		15		16		
17	18					
	19			20		

Across		Down	
2	The value of $x^3y^0z^2$ if $x = 2$, $y = 5$ and $z = -3$.	**1**	The value of x if $x = 2(10y + 1)$ and $y + 2x = 209$.
4	$11 - \frac{2x - 3}{5} = 26 - x$	**3**	The value of xy if $y = 2x + 1$ and $5y - 4x = 23$.
6	The value of x if $2(x + 7) = 3 - (2 - 3x)$.	**5**	The value of $xz^2 + 3x^3y$ if $x = 2$, $y = -1$ and $z = 6$.
8	The value of x^2y if $x = -5$ and $y = 9$.	**7**	The value of x if $x - 3y = 4$ and $x + y = 40$.
10	The value of x if $5 - \frac{3x - 15}{7} = 2$.	**9**	The value of x if $\frac{x}{9} - 16 = 40$.
12	The value of x^4 if $x = -3$.	**11**	The value of x if $x + 45 = 3(x - 5) + 4$.
15	The value of x if $\frac{x + 8}{11} - 3 = 37$.	**13**	The value of x if $10^x = 10\,000\,000\,000$.
17	The value of xy if $y = 3x - 2$ and $5x - 2y = 1$.	**14**	The value of x if $2(49 - x) = x - 28$.
19	The value of x if $2^x = 1024$.	**16**	The value of xy if $x + 2y = 60$ and $2x - y = 100$.
20	The value of y if $y - 3x = 500$ and $3y + x = 2500$.	**18**	The value of x if $6 - 2(x - 9) = 3(x - 10) - 1$.

ISBN: 9780170447096

Challenge 5

For each of the following, define a variable, if necessary, write one or more equations and solve in order to answer the question.

1 Three cartons of popcorn and two ice creams cost \$14. An ice cream costs 50c less than a carton of popcorn. Calculate the cost of a carton of popcorn and the cost of an ice cream.

____

____

____

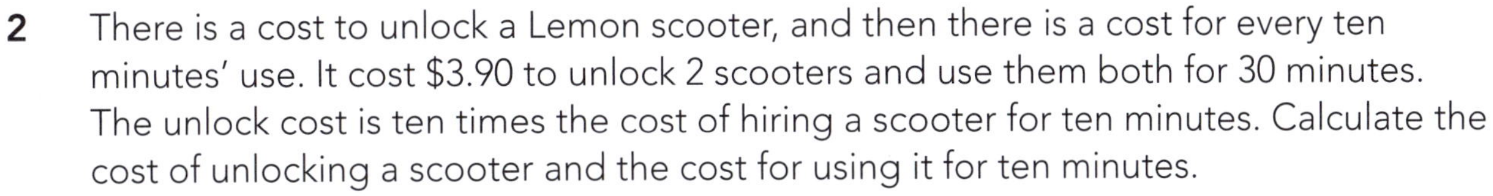

2 There is a cost to unlock a Lemon scooter, and then there is a cost for every ten minutes' use. It cost \$3.90 to unlock 2 scooters and use them both for 30 minutes. The unlock cost is ten times the cost of hiring a scooter for ten minutes. Calculate the cost of unlocking a scooter and the cost for using it for ten minutes.

____

____

____

3 A fifth of the difference between double a number and three is the same as the difference between 39 and quadruple the number. What is the number?

____

____

____

4 A triangle has sides with the following lengths, in centimetres: $\frac{2x-5}{3}$, $x-3$ and $x-2$. A square has sides that are $\frac{x+2}{3}$ cm long. If the figures have equal perimeters, calculate the lengths of their sides.

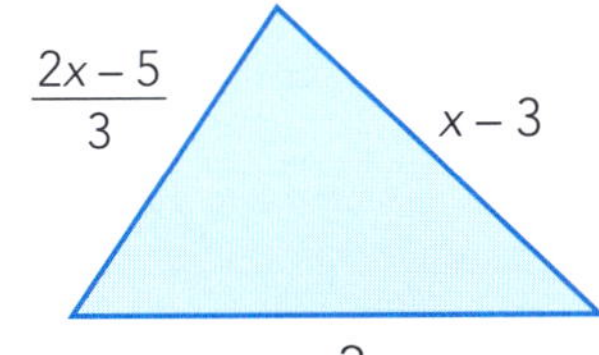

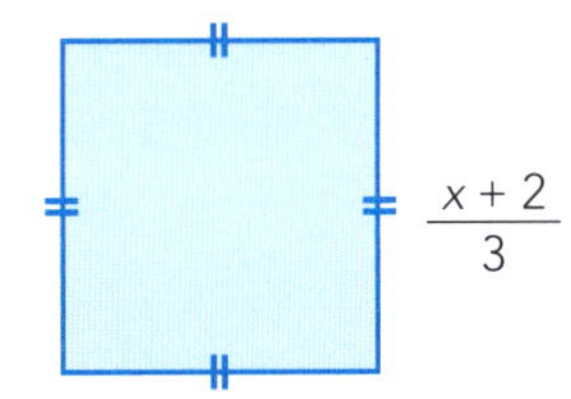

____

____

____

ISBN: 9780170447096

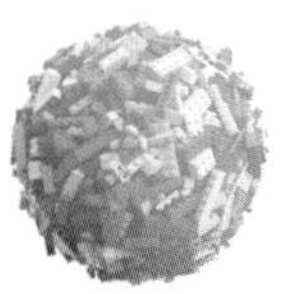

Quadratic expressions

- Up until now, you have dealt only with equations where the highest power of the variable is 1 (e.g. $2x^1 + 7 = 11$).
- These are known as **linear** expressions, because their graphs form **straight lines**.
- An expression in which the highest power of the variable is 2 (e.g. x^2) is known as a **quadratic** expression.
- Usually these contain an x^2, but in factorised form quadratic expressions may look like $(x \pm a)(x \pm b)$ or $x(x \pm a)$.
- When graphed, quadratics form curves known as **parabolas**:

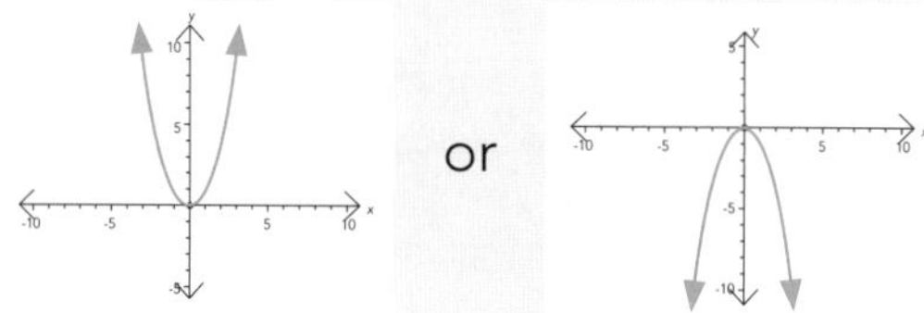

Expanding quadratic expressions

Remember **FOIL:**

Multiply the **F**irsts, **O**uters, **I**nners, **L**asts.

F O I L

e.g. $(x + 2)(x - 5) = x^2 - 5x + 2x - 10$

$= x^2 - 3x - 10$

Combine like terms.

Examples:

1 $(x + 7)(x + 5) = x^2 + 5x + 7x + 35$

$= x^2 + 12x + 35$

2 $(x + 12)^2 = (x + 12)(x + 12)$

$= x^2 + 12x + 12x + 144$

$= x^2 + 24x + 144$

3 $(x - 5)^2 = (x - 5)(x - 5)$

$= x^2 - 5x - 5x + 25$

$= x^2 - 10x + 25$

4 $(x + 5)(x - 5) = x^2 - 5x + 5x - 25$

$= x^2 - 25$

Look for the pattern here. Be careful!

5 $(2x - 3)(x + 7) = 2x^2 + 14x - 3x - 21$

$= 2x^2 + 11x - 21$

 ISBN: 9780170447096

Expand and simplify these.

1 $(x + 5)(x + 1) =$ ______

$= x^2 + \square\, x + 5$

2 $(x - 3)(x + 7) =$ ______

$= x^2 + \square\, x \,\square\, 21$

3 $(x - 9)(x + 1) =$ ______

$= x^2 \,\square\,\square\, x - 9$

4 $(x - 4)(x - 8) =$ ______

$= x^2 \,\square\,\square\, x + 32$

5 $(x + 7)^2 =$ ______

$= x^2 + \square\, x + 49$

6 $(x - 6)^2 =$ ______

$= x^2 - \square\, x \,\square\, 36$

7 $(x + 10)(x - 10) =$ ______

$=$ ______

$= x^2 + \square\, x \,\square\, 100$

8 $(x + 3)(x - 2) =$ ______

$=$ ______

$=$ ______

9 $(x - 11)(x + 8) =$ ______

$=$ ______

$=$ ______

10 $(x - 1)(x - 4) =$ ______

$=$ ______

$=$ ______

11 $(3x + 2)(x + 4) =$ ______

$=$ ______

$=$ ______

12 $(x - 1)(2x + 3) =$ ______

$=$ ______

$=$ ______

13 $(5x - 2)(x - 1) =$ ______

$=$ ______

$=$ ______

14 $(x - 7)^2 =$ ______

$=$ ______

$=$ ______

15 $(x + 6)(x - 6) =$ ______

$=$ ______

$=$ ______

16 $(2x + 1)(x - 12) =$ ______

$=$ ______

$=$ ______

ISBN: 9780170447096

Factorising quadratic expressions

Steps:

1 List all the factors of the constant: $x^2 + 3x - 40$

1, 40
2, 20
4, 10
5, 8

2 Select the pair that could add or subtract to give the coefficient of x: $x^2 + 3x - 40$

$-5 + 8 = +3$

3 The factors are $(x - 5)(x + 8)$

or $(x + 8)(x - 5)$

Check your answer by expanding the brackets using **FOIL** — you should get the original expression: $(x - 5)(x + 8) = x^2 + 3x - 40$

Examples:

1 $x^2 + 7x + 12 = (x + 3)(x + 4)$

1, 12
2, 6
3, 4

2 $x^2 - 11x + 30 = (x - 5)(x - 6)$

1, 30
2, 15
3, 10
5, 6

3 $x^2 - 7x - 18 = (x + 2)(x - 9)$

1, 18
2, 9
3, 6

4 $x^2 - 36 = x^2 + 0x - 36 = (x + 6)(x - 6)$

1, 36
2, 18
3, 12
4, 9
6, 6

Insert a 'fake' x term.

Complete the factorisations of the following.

1 $x^2 + 12x + 11 = (x +$ ☐ $)(x +$ ☐ $)$

2 $x^2 + 6x + 8 = (x +$ ☐ $)(x +$ ☐ $)$

3 $x^2 + 4x - 5 = (x$ ☐ $5)(x$ ☐ $1)$

4 $x^2 - 4x - 12 = (x$ ☐ $2)(x$ ☐ $6)$

5 $x^2 - 3x - 18 = (x$ ☐ $6)(x$ ☐ $3)$

6 $x^2 + 9x - 10 = (x$ ☐ $1)(x$ ☐ $10)$

7 $x^2 - 16x + 64 = (x$ ☐ $8)^2$

8 $x^2 - 16 = (x$ ☐ $4)(x$ ☐ $4)$

 ISBN: 9780170447096

9 $x^2 + 4x + 3 =$ ______

10 $x^2 + 18x + 17 =$ ______

11 $x^2 + 7x + 6 =$ ______

12 $x^2 + 5x + 6 =$ ______

13 $x^2 - 7x + 6 =$ ______

14 $x^2 - 5x + 6 =$ ______

15 $x^2 + 5x - 6 =$ ______

16 $x^2 - 5x - 6 =$ ______

17 $x^2 + x - 6 =$ ______

18 $x^2 - x - 6 =$ ______

19 $x^2 + 6x + 9 =$ ______

20 $x^2 + 12x + 36 =$ ______

21 $x^2 - 20x + 100 =$ ______

22 $x^2 - 49 =$ ______

23 $x^2 - 18x + 81 =$ ______

24 $x^2 - 1 =$ ______

25 $x^2 - 0.01 =$ ______

26 $x^2 - 11x + 121 =$ ______

ISBN: 9780170447096

Solving quadratic equations

1 Factorised quadratic equations

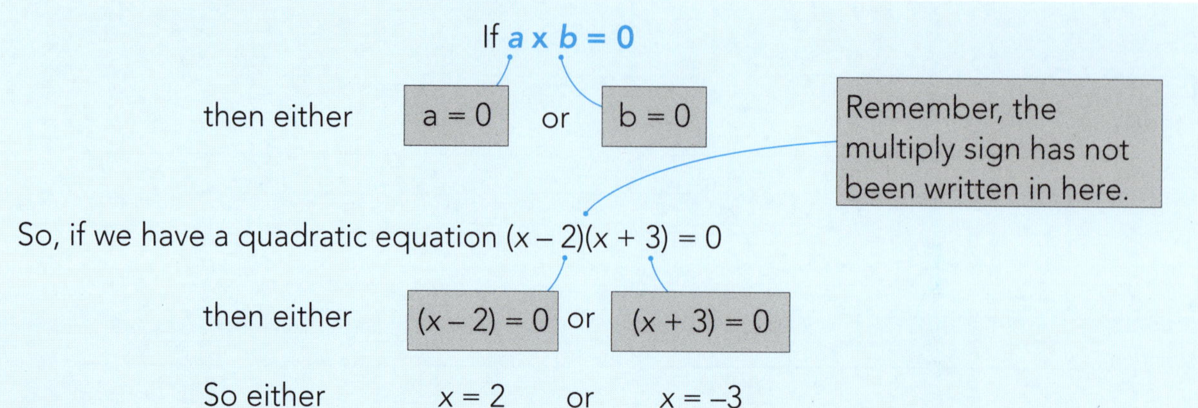

Note:

- Most quadratic equations that you come across will have two different solutions. However, some will have two identical solutions, and some will have no real solutions.
- There may be two solutions, but in practical situations, one may not work.

Examples:

1 $(x+7)(x-2) = 0$
Either $(x+7) = 0$
$\mathbf{x = -7}$
or $(x-2) = 0$
$\mathbf{x = 2}$

2 $(x+5)(x-5) = 0$
Either $(x+5) = 0$
$\mathbf{x = -5}$
or $(x-5) = 0$
$\mathbf{x = 5}$

3 $x(x+9) = 0$
Either $\mathbf{x = 0}$
or $(x+9) = 0$
$\mathbf{x = -9}$

4 $(x+3)^2 = 0$
$\therefore\ (x+3) = 0$
$\mathbf{x = -3}$

This can be considered to be one solution, or two identical solutions.

Solve the following equations.

1 $(x+3)(x+7) = 0$

____

2 $(x+2)(x+5) = 0$

____

3 $(x-6)(x+3) = 0$

____

4 $(x+1)(x-9) = 0$

____

5 $(x-11)(x+4) = 0$

____

6 $(x+5)(x-2) = 0$

____

 ISBN: 9780170447096

7 $(x + 3)(x - 7) = 0$

8 $(x - 2)(x + 6) = 0$

9 $(x - 10)(x + 4) = 0$

10 $(x + 7)(x - 7) = 0$

11 $(x - 12)^2 = 0$

12 $(x + 4)^2 = 0$

13 $(x - 8)^2 = 0$

14 $(x - 2)(x + 2) = 0$

2 Unfactorised quadratic equations

- Do this by factorising the equation first.

Example: $x^2 - 3x - 10 = 0$

Step 1: Factorise: $(x + 2)(x - 5) = 0$

Step 2: Solve by considering what happens when each bracket equals 0.

Either $(x + 2) = 0$

$\mathbf{x = -2}$

or $(x - 5) = 0$

$\mathbf{x = 5}$

So, if $x^2 - 3x - 10 = 0$, then x is either -2 or 5.

Examples:

1

$x^2 + 8x + 7 = 0$

$(x + 7)(x + 1) = 0$

Either $(x + 7) = 0$

$\mathbf{x = -7}$

or $(x + 1) = 0$

$\mathbf{x = -1}$

2

$x^2 + 2x + 1 = 0$

$(x + 1)(x + 1) = 0$

$\therefore (x + 1) = 0$

$\mathbf{x = -1}$

One solution only, or two identical solutions.

3

$x^2 - 4 = 0$

$(x + 2)(x - 2) = 0$

Either $(x + 2) = 0$

$\mathbf{x = -2}$

or $(x - 2) = 0$

$\mathbf{x = 2}$

4

$x^2 - 11x = 0$

$x(x - 11) = 0$

Either $\mathbf{x = 0}$

or $(x - 11) = 0$

$\mathbf{x = 11}$

ISBN: 9780170447096

Solve the following equations.

1 $x^2 + 4x + 3 = 0$

$x^2 + 4x + 3 = (\square)(\square) = 0$

$x = \square$ or $x = \square$

2 $x^2 + 7x + 10 = 0$

$x^2 + 7x + 10 = (\square)(\square) = 0$

$x = \square$ or $x = \square$

3 $x^2 + 3x - 28 = 0$

$x^2 + 3x - 28 = (\square)(\square) = 0$

$x = \square$ or $x = \square$

4 $x^2 - 5x + 24 = 0$

$x^2 - 5x + 24 = (\square)(\square) = 0$

$x = \square$ or $x = \square$

5 $x^2 + 13x + 36 = 0$

6 $x^2 - 6x - 55 = 0$

7 $x^2 - 10x + 16 = 0$

8 $x^2 - 2x - 24 = 0$

9 $x^2 - 11x + 18 = 0$

10 $x^2 - 30x - 64 = 0$

11 $x^2 + 4x - 21 = 0$

12 $x^2 - 5x - 36 = 0$

13 $x^2 - 49 = 0$

14 $x^2 + 16x + 64 = 0$

15 $x^2 - 13x = 0$

16 $x^2 - 9x + 20 = 0$

17 $x^2 - 13x - 30 = 0$

18 $x^2 + x = 0$

 ISBN: 9780170447096

3 Quadratic equations with a common factor

Do this by removing the common factor first.

Example: $\mathbf{2x^2 - 18x - 20 = 0}$

Notice that 2 is a common factor of each term.

Step 1: Take out the common factor: $2(x^2 - 9x - 10) = 0$

Step 2: Factorise the bracket contents: $2(x + 1)(x - 10) = 0$

Step 3: Solve in the usual manner: Either $(x + 1) = 0$

$\mathbf{x = -1}$

or $(x - 10) = 0$

$\mathbf{x = 10}$

Either $(x + 1)$ or $(x - 10)$ must equal 0.

So, if $2x^2 - 18x - 20 = 0$, then x is either -1 or 10.

Examples:

1

$3x^2 + 27x + 42 = 0$

$3(x^2 + 9x + 14) = 0$

$3(x + 2)(x + 7) = 0$

Either $(x + 2) = 0$

$\mathbf{x = -2}$

or $(x + 7) = 0$

$\mathbf{x = -7}$

2

$5x^2 + 30 + 45 = 0$

$5(x^2 + 6x + 9) = 0$

$5(x + 3)^2 = 0$

$\therefore (x + 3) = 0$

$\mathbf{x = -3}$

One solution only, or two identical solutions.

Solve the following equations.

1 $2x^2 + 12x + 10 = 0$

$2x^2 + 12x + 10 =$ ☐ $(x^2 + 6x + 5)$

$=$ ☐ (☐)(☐) $=0$

$x =$ ☐ or $x =$ ☐

2 $3x^2 - 48 = 0$

$3x^2 - 48 =$ ☐ $(x^2 - 16)$

$=$ ☐ (☐)(☐) $= 0$

$x =$ ☐ or $x =$ ☐

3 $4x^2 + 16x + 12 = 0$

____

____

4 $10x^2 + 10x - 120 = 0$

____

____

5 $3x^2 - 24x + 45 = 0$

____

____

6 $2x^2 - 6x - 36 = 0$

____

____

7 $7x^2 - 7 = 0$

____

____

8 $6x^2 + 36x + 54 = 0$

____

____

ISBN: 9780170447096

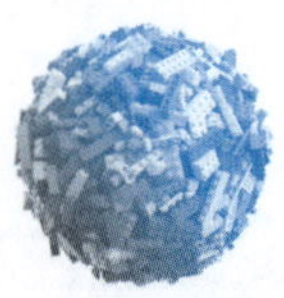

Challenge 6

Solve the following equations.

1 $2x^2 + 7x + 3 = 0$

2 $3x^2 + 5x + 2 = 0$

3 $2x^2 + 7x + 6 = 0$

4 $5x^2 + 17x + 6 = 0$

5 $2x^2 + 5x - 3 = 0$

6 $3x^2 + x - 2 = 0$

7 $7x^2 - 20x - 3 = 0$

8 $3x^2 - 14x - 5 = 0$

9 $2x^2 - 7x + 3 = 0$

10 $3x^2 - 5x + 2 = 0$

11 $4x^2 - 10x + 6 = 0$

12 $4x^2 - 1 = 0$

13 $9x^2 - 4 = 0$

14 $100x^2 - 49 = 0$

 ISBN: 9780170447096

Find the errors

Some of the following equations are solved correctly and some aren't. If the equation is solved correctly, put a tick in the ✓/✗ column. If not, put a cross in the ✓/✗ column, highlight the mistake, and write the correct solution.

		✓/✗	Correct solution
1	$5y + 3x = 1$ ① $x = 11 - 7y$ ② Substitute ② into ①: $5y + 3(11 - 7y) = 1$ $5y + 33 - 2y = 1$ $-16y = -32$ $\therefore\ y = 2$ and $x = -3$		
2	$2x^2 - 10x - 12 = 0$ $2(x^2 - 5x - 6) = 0$ $2(x - 2)(x - 3) = 0$ $\therefore\ x = 2$ or $x = 3$		
3	$4x^2 - 100 = 0$ $4(x^2 - 25) = 0$ $4(x - 5)(x + 5) = 0$ $\therefore\ x = 5$ or $x = -5$		
4	$5x + 2y = -2$ ① $2x - y = -8$ ② Multiply ② by 2 and add to ①: $4x - 2y = -16$ $9x = -18$ $\therefore\ x = -2$ and $y = 4$		
5	$x^2 - 2x - 15 = 0$ $(x + 3)(x - 5) = 0$ $\therefore\ x = 3$ or $x = -5$		

ISBN: 9780170447096

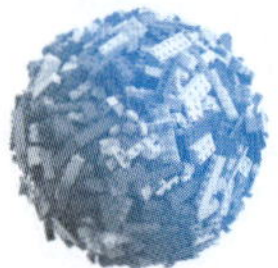

Challenge 7

Do the working needed to complete the cross-number in your exercise book.

1		2		3	4	
					5	6
		7		8		
9	10					
	11	12		13		14
15		16	17			
18			19			

Across		**Down**	
1	The product of the solutions to $x^2 - 22 + 121 = 0$.	**2**	xy if $y = 9x - 5$ and $x + 2y = 66$.
3	The coefficient of x when $(3x + 2)(x + 11)$ is expanded.	**4**	$3x$ if $5(x + 7) - 52 = 4x$.
5	$\frac{1}{2}x$ where x is the larger solution to $2x^2 - 69x + 34 = 0$.	**6**	$-8x$ where x is the smaller of the solutions to $x^2 + 14x + 45 = 0$.
7	x^2 if $25 - 2x = 3x - 80$.	**8**	The product of the solutions to $x^2 + 23x + 112 = 0$.
9	$8x$ where $2^x = 128$.	**10**	xy if $4y - 3x = 15$ and $y + x = 16$.
11	$4x^3$ if $1 - (1 - x) = 4 - x$.	**12**	Double the larger solution to $x^2 - 121 = 0$.
13	$2x^2$ if $9x - 59 = 2x + 18$.	**14**	$\frac{xy}{3}$ if $y - 2x = 26$ and $x + y = 62$.
16	The square of one of the solutions to $x^2 - 10x + 25 = 0$.	**15**	$6x$ where x is the larger root of $x^2 - 3x - 28 = 0$.
18	$-7x$ where x is the larger solution to $x^2 + 11x + 24 = 0$.	**17**	x^2y if $y = 2x$ and $5y - 7x = 9$.
19	$3x^2$ if $3^x = 81$.		

ISBN: 9780170447096

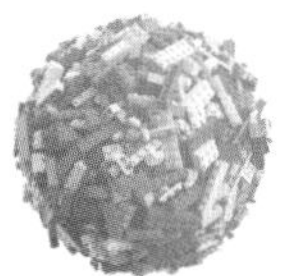

Understanding instructions in algebra

How do I recognise when to ...?	Example	What do I do?	What should the answer look like?
Solve	**Linear** $5x + 4 = 18 - 2x$ Contains an '=' sign.	If linear, shift terms with variables to the left, and constants to the right. $5x + 4 = 18 - 2x$ $(+ 2x)$ $7x + 4 = 18$ $(- 4)$ $7x = 14$ $(\div 7)$ $x = 2$	Variable = constant. $x = 2$
	Inequation $3x - 2 \leq -20$ Contains one of these signs: >, <, ≤ or ≥.	Same rules as for linear equations except: if you multiply both sides by a negative number or flip the sides, then reverse the sign. $3x - 2 \leq -20$ $3x \leq -18$ $x \leq -6$	One of the following: variable < constant variable > constant variable ≤ constant variable ≥ constant. $x \leq -6$
	Quadratic $x^2 - 2x - 15 = 0$ Contains an '=' sign.	Factorise, then make each factor = 0. $(x - 5)(x + 3) = 0$ Either $(x - 5) = 0$, so $x = 5$ or $(x + 3) = 0$, so $x = -3$	Variable = one or two constants. $x = 5$ or -3
	Exponential $2^x = 32$ Contains an '=' sign.	List the powers of the base until you find the value you need. $2^2 = 4$, $2^3 = 8$, $2^4 = 16$, $2^5 = 32$. So $x = 5$	Variable = constant. $x = 5$
Evaluate	$2x^2 - 3x$ when $x = 5$ You are told the value of a variable.	Substitute the value for the variable. $2x^2 - 3x = 2(5)^2 + 3(5)$ $= 50 - 15$ $= 35$	A constant. 35

ISBN: 9780170447096

How do I recognise when to ...?	Example	What do I do?	What should the answer look like?
Expand	**One bracket** $2p^2(5p + q^2 - 1)$ Contains **brackets.**	If linear, multiply every term that is inside the brackets by the term outside. $2p^2(5p + q^2 - 1)$ $= 10p^3 + 2p^2q^2 - 2p^2$	An expression with no brackets. $10p^3 + 2p^2q^2 - 2p^2$
	Two brackets $(2x + 3)(x - 7)$ Contains **brackets.**	Use FOIL, then collect like terms. $2x^2 - 14x + 3x - 21$ $= 2x^2 - 11x - 21$	An expression with no brackets. $2x^2 - 11x - 21$
Simplify	**Adding/subtracting** $3p^2 + pq + p^2 - 2pq - 6$ Contains a mixture of like and unlike terms.	Combine like terms. $3p^2 + \underline{pq} + p^2 - \underline{2pq} - 6$ $= 4p^2 - pq - 6$	An expression containing no like terms. $4p^2 - pq - 6$
	Multiplying/dividing $\frac{12ab^5}{3a^3bc}$ The same variable occurs in more than one place.	Add or subtract indices for each variable that occurs more than once. $\frac{12ab^5}{3a^3bc} = \frac{4b^4}{a^2c}$	An expression in which each variable occurs no more than once. $\frac{4b^4}{a^2c}$
Factorise	**Not a quadratic** $20a^2b - 5ab$ Several added or subtracted terms containing common factors.	Put the common factor outside the bracket. Divide each term by the common factor to find what goes inside the brackets. $20a^2b - 5ab = 5ab(4a - 1)$	An expression with brackets. **No common factors inside the brackets.** $5ab(4a - 1)$
	Quadratic $x^2 - x - 12$ A squared term, usually a term with a variable, and a constant.	See page 66. $(x - 4)(x + 3)$	An expression with two sets of brackets. **No common factors inside the brackets.** $(x - 4)(x + 3)$

 ISBN: 9780170447096

Write the most appropriate instruction (**Solve**, **Evaluate**, **Expand**, **Simplify** or **Factorise**) for each question. Then follow your chosen instruction in order to answer the question.

	Question	Instruction	Answer
1	$7p^2 - 2q + 9q - p^2 + 1$	Simplify	
2	$5 - 11x = 4x - 55$		
3	$5x^2y + 20xy^2$		
4	$\frac{8x^2y^6}{12x^3y}$		
5	$(x - 7)(x + 11) = 0$		
6	$x^3 - 10x - 3x^2$, where $x = 3$		
7	$\frac{5x - 7}{2} = x + 4$		
8	$x^2 - 2x - 3 = 0$		

ISBN: 9780170447096

	Question	Instruction	Answer
9	$-2p(p^2 - 3p - 9)$		
10	$5x^2y$, if $x = 0.4$ and $y = 2$		
11	$3^x = 81$		
12	$3 - 7x < x + 19$		
13	$15pq^3(2q - p^2)$		
14	$6ab^3c \times 2a^4bc$		
15	$10^x = 10\,000$		
16	$x^2 + 6x - 27$		
17	$4x^2 - 64 = 0$		
18	$(3x + 7)(x - 2)$		

ISBN: 9780170447096

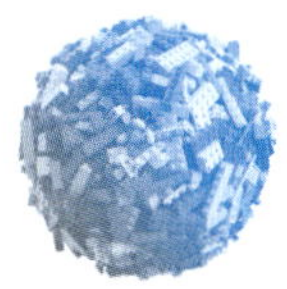

Revision 1

1 Write an expression for this phrase. Use the variable *y*.

23 less than half a number: ________

2 Write a phrase for this expression.

$\frac{5-x}{3}$: ________________________

3 When sausages are ordered for the school camp, they have found that they need eight sausages for the staff, and two sausages per student plus one spare sausage for every three students. The formula for the total number of sausages needed is given by the expression **Total = 8 + 2s +** $\frac{s}{3}$.

a The variable is ____ and it stands for ______________________________.

b Use the expression to calculate how many sausages will be needed if there are 36 students.

____

4 Simplify the following expressions.

a $5p^5 \times p =$ ________________

b $2d^3ef \times 3de^4f^4 =$ ________________

c $3d^0 \times d^0 =$ ________________

d $f^2 - e + f + 2f^2 - 2e =$ ________________

e $\frac{6a^3bc^8}{4a^3b^2c^4} =$ ________________

____

f $\frac{a^2bc^0}{3ab^5} =$ ________________

____

g $2(10p^5q^0)^4 =$ ________________

____

h $\frac{12z^5}{4z^3} - 3z^2 =$ ________________

____

5 Expand the following expressions.

a $5z(3y + 2x^2) =$ ________________

b $-2pq(6 - 3p) =$ ________________

6 Factorise the following expressions.

a $24qr + 8r =$ ________________

b $-15s^2t^2 - 6s^2t =$ ________________

7 Complete the table.

Formula	$d = 6, e = 2$	$d = 3, e = 6$	$d = -3, e = 4$	$d = -5, e = -3$
$A = de - 3e^2$	A = ________	A = ________	A = ________	A = ________

ISBN: 9780170447096

8 Solve the following equations.

a $23 = 35 - 6p$

b $4 + \frac{x}{3} = x - 4$

c $2 - x = 1 + \frac{3 - 4x}{5}$

d $f + 15 = 7f - 3$

e $8 - 2(6 - z) = 4(2z + 5)$

f $3(3 - x) \geq 1 + x$

g $3 - \frac{x - 1}{2} < 5 + x$

h $10^x = 100\,000\,000$

i $y = 2x + 1$
$3y - x = 18$

j $5 - 4x = 3y$
$7 + x = 2y$

9 Write and solve equations for each of the following. Use x as your variable.

a Seven is equal to half of the difference between triple a number and four.

b Five less than a quarter of a number is the same as one more than the number.

c Three consecutive multiples of three add to 45. What are the three numbers?

 ISBN: 9780170447096

10 Angus is saving up for a new phone, which will cost him \$360. He has \$110 in the bank, and he can earn \$12 for each hour he works in his neighbour's garden. Write an inequation to represent this situation, and solve it in order to calculate the minimum number of hours that he will need to work before he can buy the phone.

11 A hamburger costs 50c more than two drinks. Four hamburgers and three drinks cost \$35. Let y represent the price of a hamburger, and x represent the price of a drink. Write equations for each statement, and solve them simultaneously in order to find the prices of hamburgers and drinks.

12 Answer the following.

a Expand and simplify $(2x - 5)(x + 4)$

b Factorise $x^2 - 7x - 18$

c Solve $(x + 3)(x - 9) = 0$

d Solve $x^2 + x - 12 = 0$

e Solve $x^2 - 36 = 0$

f Solve $2x^2 - 12x + 16 = 0$

13 Write the most appropriate instruction (Solve, Evaluate, Expand, Simplify or Factorise) for each question. Then follow your chosen instruction in order to answer the question.

	Question	Instruction	Answer
a	$p^2 - 12p - 28 = 0$		
b	$(2t)^3 - s$ if $t = -1$ and $s = 7$		

ISBN: 9780170447096

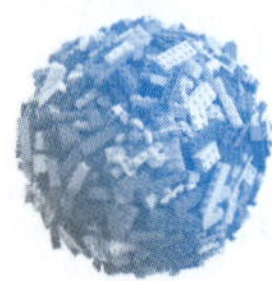

Revision 2

1 Write an expression for this phrase. Use the variable y. The square of five less than a number: ______

2 Write a phrase for this expression:

$\frac{2x-1}{3}$: ______

3 At the school camp, they must have enough radios to give one to each of the three staff members, and one to each group of four students. The formula for the total number of radios needed is given by the expression **Total** $= \frac{s}{4} + 3$.

a The variable is ____ and it stands for ______.

b Use the expression to calculate how many radios they will need if there are 36 students.

______

4 Simplify the following expressions.

a $p^5 \times 3p^2 \times 2 =$ ______

b $7a^2b^6c^0 \times 2a^5b =$ ______

c $5 + 3d^0 =$ ______

d $4x^2y - 2xy - 3yx^2 + 5 =$ ______

e $12g^2h^4 \div 4g^3h^5 =$ ______

f $\frac{5p^5}{20p^7q^5} =$ ______

g $(3(2p^3)^2)^2 =$ ______

h $\frac{4a^3}{a^2} + \frac{6a^2}{3a} =$ ______

5 Expand the following expressions.

a $7y(4y^2 + 3) =$ ______

b $-4p(p^2 - 3q) =$ ______

6 Factorise the following expressions.

a $12w + 20vw =$ ______

b $-15m^4n^2 + 3mn =$ ______

7 Complete the table.

Formula	$d = 5, e = 2$	$d = 3, e = 5$	$d = -2, e = 10$	$d = -1, e = -3$
$A = d^2e - 5e^2$	$A =$ ______	$A =$ ______	$A =$ ______	$A =$ ______

ISBN: 9780170447096

8 Solve the following equations.

a $7 = 23 - 4p$

b $2 + x = \frac{x}{4} - 1$

c $\frac{3x - 2}{2} + 5 = 9 - x$

d $4 - 3f = 10 + 7f$

e $3(2z - 1) + 4 = 2 - (3 - z)$

f $9 - x < 3 + 2x$

g $5 - x \leq 1 + \frac{x}{3}$

h $10^x = 100\,000$

i $3x - 4y = 19$
$x + 2y = 3$

j $x = 3y + 1$
$2x - y = 12$

9 Write and solve equations for each of the following. Use x as your variable.

a One more than a quarter of the difference between five times a number and seven is the same as two less than the number.

b When two thirds of a number is reduced by seven, the result is the same as subtracting twelve from the number.

c When ten is subtracted from the sum of three consecutive odd numbers, the answer is 53. What are the three numbers?

10 Mel is planting beans. She needs four stakes for the first row, and two stakes for each additional row. She has 29 stakes. Write an inequation to represent this situation, and solve it in order to calculate the maximum number of rows of beans that she can plant.

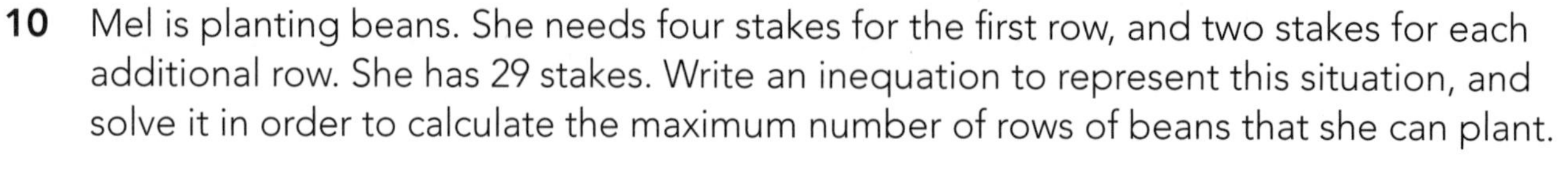

11 A piece of fish costs \$8 less than two cheeseburgers. Five pieces of fish and four cheeseburgers cost \$58. Let *y* represent the price of a cheeseburger, and *x* represent the price of a piece of fish. Write equations for each statement, and solve them simultaneously in order to find the prices of cheeseburgers and pieces of fish.

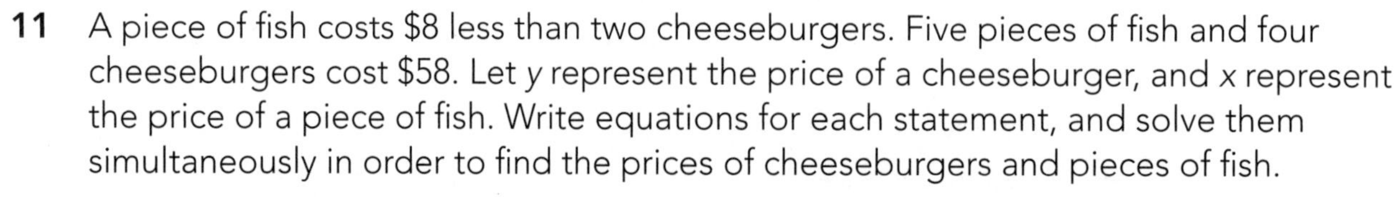

12 Answer the following.

a Expand and simplify $(x + 2)(3x - 11)$

b Factorise $x^2 - 15x + 36$

c Solve $(x - 7)(x + 12) = 0$

d Solve $x^2 - 11x + 24 = 0$

e Solve $x^2 + 10x + 25 = 0$

f Solve $3x^2 + 21x - 24 = 0$

13 Write the most appropriate instruction (Solve, Evaluate, Expand, Simplify or Factorise) for each question. Then follow your chosen instruction in order to answer the question.

	Question	Instruction	Answer
a	$x^2 - 2x + 1$		
b	$2 - (7x - 6) = 3(x + 1)$		

  ISBN: 9780170447096

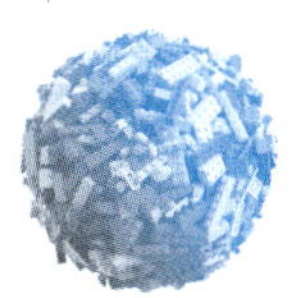

Answers

Revision (pp. 6–10)

Simplifying expressions (pp. 6–7)

Multiplying

1 p^2 2 ghm
3 $4c$ 4 $12fg$
5 $-5w$ 6 $9fg$

Dividing

7 $2g$ 8 $\frac{5p}{n}$
9 $\frac{4}{f}$ 10 $4f$
11 $3c$ 12 $\frac{1}{2g}$

Putting it together

1 $\frac{b}{2}$ 2 $20a$
3 $\frac{1}{8d}$ 4 $4pq$
5 $10mn$ 6 $\frac{3}{e}$
7 $2a$ 8 $-12b$
9 $7jk$ 10 $\frac{7}{a}$

Like terms (p. 8)

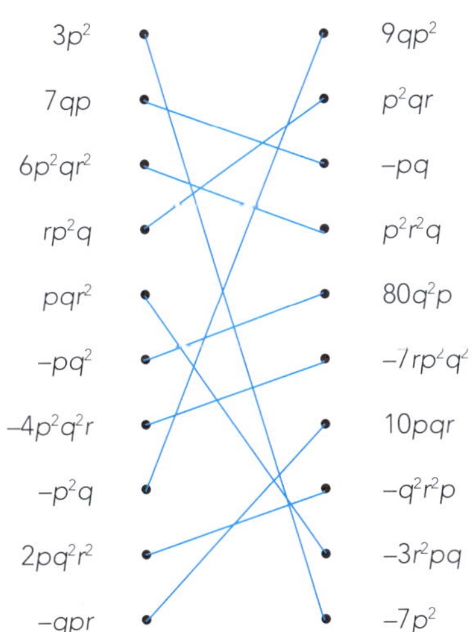

Adding and subtracting (p. 9)

1 $4y$ 2 $10a$
3 $8x$ 4 $4y$
5 $6y + x$ 6 $x + 3$
7 $6y - 2x$ 8 $7m + n$
9 $2x + 3y + 2$ 10 $3p + 4q + 11$
11 $4a + 7b$ 12 $7x + 3$
13 $-f - 15g$ 14 $p^2 + 3p$
15 $14x^2 - 3x + 7$ 16 $p^2 - 3q^2 + 10$

Mixing it up (p. 10)

1 $\frac{1}{4}$ 2 $4g - 7fg$
3 $3d$ 4 $12p^2q^2$
5 $4x^2 + 6x - 1$ 6 $\frac{1}{3y}$
7 $7ab - 2b^2 - 4b$ 8 $\frac{x}{5}$
9 $\frac{a}{2}$ 10 $-z - 2z^2 + 2yz$
11 $30f^2g^2$ 12 $\frac{5}{9}$
13 $\frac{ac}{5}$ 14 $4p^2 - 5p - 1$
15 $-4m$ 16 $\frac{5mn}{2}$
17 $2pq$ 18 $8c^2d$
19 $\frac{a}{7c}$ 20 $10a + ab^2 - 3b + b^2$

The language of algebra (pp. 11–15)

Words to operations (p. 11)

1 + 2 +
3 x 4 –
5 x 6 –
7 – 8 ÷
9 – 10 ÷
11 – 12 +
13 x 14 –
15 + 16 +
17 – 18 +
19 x 20 +

Phrases to expressions (pp. 12–14)

1 $4b + 2$ 2 $2(b - 4)$
3 $b + 3c$ 4 $4 + \frac{b}{2}$
5 $(b - 4)^2$ 6 $(2c)^2$
7 $\frac{4 + b}{2}$ 8 $2b - 4$
9 $4^2 - b$ 10 $(4 - b)^2$
11 $\frac{b - 4}{3}$ 12 $3(b + c)$
13 $\frac{b}{3} - 4$ 14 $b^2 - 4$
15 $4(b + 2)$ 16 $2c^2$

Check with your teacher if your answer for any questions below is different.

17 $3y + 7$ or $3(y + 7)$ 18 $3y + 7$
19 $\frac{y}{4} - 3$ or $\frac{y - 3}{4}$ 20 $\frac{y - 3}{4}$

ISBN: 9780170447096

21 $\frac{y}{2} + 3$ or $\frac{y+3}{2}$ **22** $\frac{y}{2} + 3$

23 $2y - 9$ **24** $(9 - y)^2$

Check with your teacher if your answer for any questions below is different.

25 Double b plus seven.
26 Double the sum of b and seven.
27 Five minus a third of b.
28 A third of the difference between five and b.
29 A quarter of a number, plus seven.
30 A quarter of the sum of b and seven.
31 The square of the difference between seven and b.
32 b squared less than seven.

More about variables (p. 15)

1 **a** The variable is v and it stands for **the number of visits**.
b 33 lollies

2 **a** The variable is p and it stands for **the number of pages**
b \$6.50

3 **a** The variable is m and it stands for **the number of metres added to its length**.
b 16 posts

Powers (pp. 16–19)

Multiplying powers (p. 16)

1 $2b^4$ **2** $6a^5$
3 p^4 **4** a^9
5 b^3 **6** e^6f^4
7 2 **8** $8a^4b^6$
9 $30p^5$ **10** $24a^5b^4c$

Dividing powers (p. 17)

1 $6a^{10}$ **2** $\frac{b^4}{3a^6}$
3 $\frac{1}{y^3}$ **4** $\frac{3y^8}{2}$
5 x^3y^6 **6** $\frac{f}{3e}$
7 $\frac{p}{3q}$ **8** $\frac{4}{5x^3y^8}$

Powers of powers (p. 18)

1 $25f^8$ **2** $9by^{20}z^8$
3 $8b^{15}$ **4** 1
5 $16x^6y^2$ **6** $125x^6y^{12}$
7 $7a^6b^2c^{10}$ **8** $40p^{12}q^6$
9 1 **10** $576d^{18}e^{24}$
11 $49a^6$ **12** $64p^{10}q^{12}$

Mixing it up (p. 19)

1 $2c^{12}$ **2** d^{16}
3 y^{10} **4** $3p^8$
5 $\frac{1}{c^6}$ **6** 1
7 e^{12} **8** $16g^{12}$
9 $4s^5$ **10** $9g^2$
11 6 **12** $\frac{1}{2z}$
13 $\frac{d^2}{e}$ **14** ab^8
15 $54p^6q^{15}$ **16** $9p^9$

There are a number of possible answers for the next three questions. Please check yours with your teacher.

17 $(b^3)^4$, $\frac{b^{20}}{b^8}$, $b \times b^{11}$, etc.

18 $(3y^4)^2$, $\frac{36y^{10}}{4y^2}$, $9y \times y^7$, $9(y^2)^4$, etc.

19 $(g^3h^2)^2$, $gh \times g^5h^3$, $\frac{g^{10}h^7}{g^4h^3}$, etc.

Challenge 1 (p. 20)

1 $A = 6b^3$ **2** $A = 25d^4$
3 $L = 4ab^3$ **4** $L = 4ab^3$
5 $A = 9p^3q$ **6** $H = bc^2$
7 **a** $V = 125d^9$
b $SA = 150d^6$

Challenge 2 (p. 21)

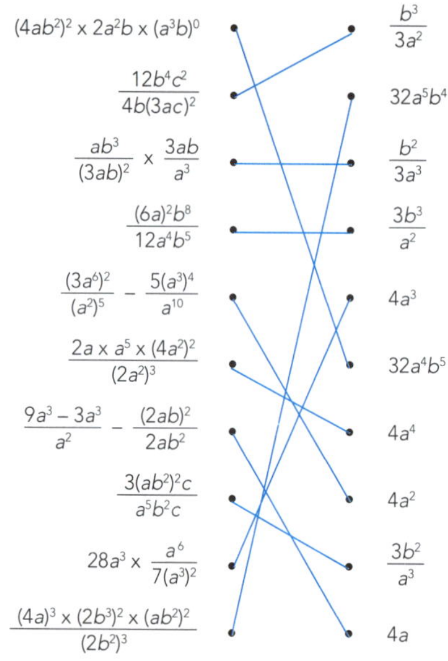

Find the errors (p. 22)

	✗/✓	Explanation	Correct solution
1	✗	Indices should be added, not multiplied.	d^5
2	✗	When adding like terms, the indices should stay the same.	$5m^2 - 5m$
3	✓		
4	✓		

 ISBN: 9780170447096

5	✗	When terms with powers are divided, the powers should be subtracted, not divided.	$5s^2t^8$
6	✗	z means z^1, so adding indices means that $z^7 \times z^1 = z^8$.	$12y^7z^8$
7	✗	q means q^1, so subtracting indices means that $q^4 \div q^1 = q^3$.	$4p^4q^3$
8	✗	$c^0 = 1$, so $(c^0)^3 = 1$	$27a^3b^6$
9	✓		
10	✓		

Brackets (pp. 23–28)

Expanding (pp. 23–24)

1 $2x^2 - 10xy + 6x$
2 $3x^2 - 3x$
3 $11y - 22$
4 $2 - x$
5 $3x^3 - 3x^2$
6 $x^2 - 2x$
7 $20x - 30$
8 $40x^2 - 35x$
9 $c - 6$
10 $-8ax - 16a$
11 $2a^4 + 6a^3b - 14a^3$
12 $3xy - 3y^2 + 15yz$
13 $12x^3 - 2x^2$
14 $6x^5 - 12x^2$
15 $3y - 2z + 4$
16 $3ab - 5a - 4$
17 $-3x^2 + 18x - 10$
18 $10a - a^3 + 5a^2$
19 $7x^3 + x^2 - 17x + 7$
20 $18a^4 - 32a^2 - 2a$

Factorising (pp. 25–27)

A

1 **1**
2 1, 7, x, **$7x$**
3 1, 5, x, **$5x$**
4 1, 3, x, x^2, $3x$, **$3x^2$**
5 1, 2, 4, 8, y, $2y$, $4y$, **$8y$**
6 1, x, y, z, xy, yz, xz, **xyz**

B

1 4
2 3
3 5
4 $5x$
5 xy
6 $3x$
7 4
8 x
9 xy^2
10 yz, $3x$

C

1 $5y$
2 3
3 $7x$
4 5
5 $4x$
6 $6z$
7 $4x^2$
8 -2
9 x
10 $5xy$

D

1 $9x + 5$
2 $x + 3$
3 $5 - x + 2y$
4 $10x^2 + 2x - 5$
5 $8x + 5 + 12y$
6 $4x - 3y$
7 $2x + 9 - x^2$
8 $5x^3 - 3$
9 $3x + 5 + x^4$
10 $x^2 - 3y$

E

1 $2(4 - x)$
2 $3x(x - 4y)$
3 $2(5x^2 - 10x - 4)$
4 $abc(1 - a + b)$

F

1 $6x(3 - 4x)$
2 $2xy(5 + 3z)$
3 $3x(4x^4 + 2 - 5x)$
4 $4(c^3 - 2c + 3)$
5 $7w(w^3 + 3 - 2w)$
6 $5pq^3(5pq - 7)$
7 $3a(5b^4 + 3a^2 - 4b)$
8 $6j(5j^4k - j + 2k^9)$
9 $m^3n^2(m^3n + n^3 - 3m^4)$
10 $2h(3g^2h^4 + 4g^3 - 12h)$
11 $-fh(g^2h^2 + 6f^4g^2 + 3h^2)$
12 $5rst(12s^2t^9 + 3rs - 2t^2)$

Find the errors (p. 28)

	✓/✗	Correct solution
1	✗	$6d - 4$
2	✓	
3	✓	
4	✗	$e(d - 36d^2 + 11)$
5	✓	
6	✓	
7	✓	
8	✗	$18d^2e^2(2d - e)$
9	✗	$d^2e^3(d^3 - e - d^2f + d^4e^5)$
10	✓	

Challenge 3 (p. 29)

1

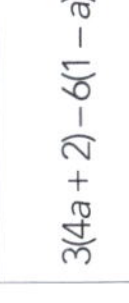

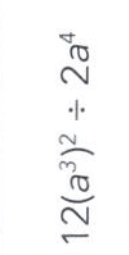

ISBN: 9780170447096

2

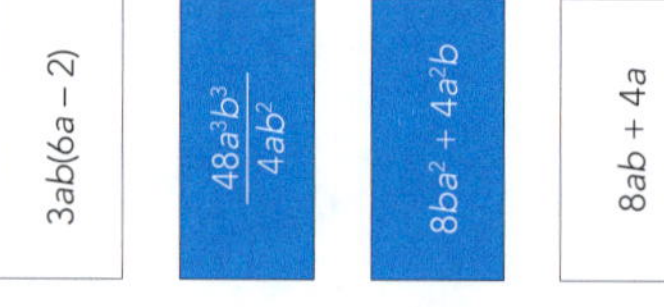

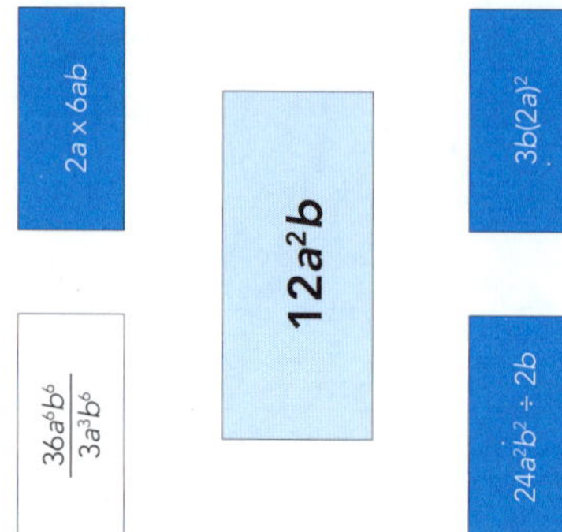

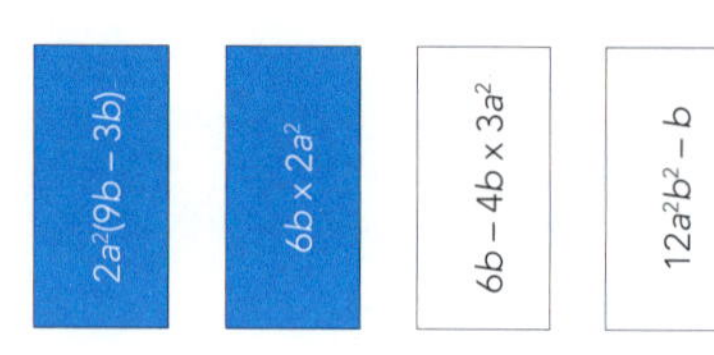

Formulae and substitution (pp. 30–34)

1 **a** $SA = 1.74\text{ m}^2$, $V = 0.135\text{ m}^3$
b $SA = 2400\text{ cm}^2$, $V = 8000\text{ cm}^3$

2 **a** $A = 90\text{ cm}^2$
b $A = 60\text{ cm}^2$

3

Formula	$b = 2$, $c = -3$	$b = -1$, $c = 4$	$b = -4$, $c = -2$
$A = 4b + 3c$	–1	8	–22
$A = 7 - 5bc$	37	27	–33
$A = -b(c - 4)$	14	0	–24
$A = c + (b - c)^2$	22	29	2
$A = 2b^2 - 5(c - 2)$	33	–8	52
$A = \frac{5b + c^2}{2}$	9.5	5.5	–8

An investigation (pp. 33–34)

km/h	11	22	33	44
m/s	3	6	9	12
energy (j)	4500	18 000	40 500	72 000

1 **d** four times the energy released by a car travelling at 11 km/h hitting a stationary object. So multiplying the velocity by **2** means the energy released in multiplied by **4**.

2 The energy released when a car travelling at 33 km/h hits a stationary object is **9** times the energy released by a car travelling at 11 km/h. So multiplying the velocity by **3** means the energy released is multiplied by **9**.

3 The energy released when a car travelling at 44 km/h hits a stationary object is **16** times the energy released by a car travelling at 11 km/h. So multiplying the velocity by **4** means the energy released is multiplied by **16**.

4

If the velocity is multiplied by	then the energy is multiplied by
2	4
3	9
4	16
a	a^2

Challenge 4 (p. 35)

	✓/✗	Correct solution
1	✓	
2	✗	–2
3	✗	70
4	✗	44
5	✓	
6	✓	
7	✗	0.24
8	✓	
9	✗	6.5

Solving linear equations (pp. 36–52)

Two-step equations (pp. 36–39)

1 $x = -3$
2 $a = 11$
3 $y = -3.5$
4 $z = -3$
5 $p = 0.5$
6 $d = -0.25$
7 $k = -4$
8 $k = -7$
9 $t = 5.5$
10 $g = -1$
11 $a = -5$
12 $x = -3$
13 $3x - 7 = 38$
$x = 15$
14 $2x - 11 = 20$
$x = 4.5$
15 $8x - 3 = 9$
$x = 1.5$
16 $7x + 5.4 = 4$
$x = -0.2$
17 $3p - 1 = 14$
Pene is 5
18 $6p = 71 + 4$
\$12.50
19 $80x + 15 = 63$
60c
20 $3h + 60 = 73.5$
4.5 hours
21 $12(x + 0.5) = 24$
$x = 1.5$
22 $12x + 16 = 46$
$x = 2.5$
Dimensions: 5 cm by 3 cm by 3.5 cm
23 $3x + 60 = 180$
$x = 40$
Angles: 80°, 70° and 30°
24 $-6x = -30$
$x = 5$
Angles: 90°, 55° and 35°

ISBN: 9780170447096

Equations with fractions (pp. 40–42)

1 $k = 49$
2 $x = 6$
3 $x = 12$
4 $x = -7$
5 $x = -5$
6 $x = 6$
7 $x = -18$
8 $x = 2$
9 $x = 0$
10 $x = -2.5$
11 $x = 1.5$
12 $x = -2$
13 $\frac{x}{2} - 7 = 5$
$x = 24$
14 $\frac{2x+5}{3} = 7$
$x = 8$
15 $\frac{3x-10}{2} = 4$
$x = 6$
16 $\frac{3x+7}{5} = 2.5$
$x = 6$
17 $\frac{20b+12}{3} = 34$
He paid \$4.50 per bag.
18 $\frac{125+4b}{3} = 59$
She paid them \$13 per bed.

Equations with variables on both sides (pp. 43–45)

1 $x = -2$
2 $y = -5$
3 $b = -8.5$
4 $a = -2.5$
5 $x = -3$
6 $c = -2.4$
7 $p = -0.7$
8 $f = 8.5$
9 $x = 2$
10 $x = -1$
11 $4x + 7 = x - 14$
$x = -7$
12 $13 - x = 2x - 5$
$x = 6$
13 $\frac{x}{3} = 2x - 5$
$x = 3$
14 $\frac{x}{2} = 14 - 3x$
$x = 4$
15 $2x + 16 = 5x - 5$
$x = 7$

Equations with brackets (pp. 46–48)

1 $x = -2.5$
2 $x = 5$
3 $x = -3.5$
4 $x = -3.5$
5 $x = 2.4$
6 $x = 0.5$
7 $x = -10$
8 $x = 0.2$
9 $x = -2$
10 $x = -6$
11 $x = 58$
12 $x = -6$
13 $x = -1$
14 $x = 1$
15 Pyramid edges: 9 cm
Cube edges: 6 cm

Inequations (pp. 49–51)

1 $x > 2$
2 $x < 9$
3 $x \geq -4$
4 $x \leq -2$
5 $x > -2$
6 $x \leq -3$
7 $x < 6$
8 $x > -2.4$
9 $x > -8$
10 $x < -6$
11 $x > -5$
12 $x \leq -2$
13 $12h \geq 156$
$h \geq 13$
She must work for at least 13 hours.
14 $59 + x \leq 80$
$x \leq 21$
Maximum luggage weight is 21 kg.
15 $65 + 29 + x \leq 118$
$x \leq 24$
Maximum width is 24 cm.
16 $23 + 2x \leq 88$
$x \leq 32.5$
Maximum amount spent on each is \$32.50.
17 $50 + 9p \leq 1000$
$p \leq 105.5$
Maximum number of pavers is 105.
18 $50 + 4x > 400$
$x > 87.5$
They need to sell at least 88 tickets.

Find the errors (p. 52)

		✓/✗	Correct solution
1	$\frac{3x-2}{5} - 8 = x + 3$ $3x - 2 - 8 = 5x + 15$ $5x + 15 = 3x - 10$ $2x = -5$ $x = -2.5$	✗	$\frac{3x-2}{5} - 8 = x + 3$ $3x - 2 - \mathbf{40} = 5x + 15$ $5x + 15 = 3x - 42$ $2x = -57$ $x = -28.5$
2	$8(2x - 1) + 3 = 5 - 4(5x + 1)$ $16x - 8 + 3 = 5 - 20x - 4$ $36x = 6$ $x = \frac{1}{6}$	✓	
3	$4(5 - 2x) - 6 \leq 3x - 8$ $20 - 8x - 6 \leq 3x - 8$ $3x - 8 \leq 14 - 8x$ $11x \leq 22$ $x \leq 2$	✗	$4(5 - 2x) - 6 \leq 3x - 8$ $20 - 8x - 6 \leq 3x - 8$ $3x - 8 \boldsymbol{\geq} 14 - 8x$ $11x \geq 22$ $x \geq 2$
4	$5(2x - 3) = \frac{3x+4}{2}$ $10(4x - 6) = 3x + 4$ $40x - 60 = 3x + 4$ $37x = 64$ $x = \frac{64}{37}$	✗	$5(2x - 3) = \frac{3x+4}{2}$ $10(\mathbf{2x - 3}) = 3x + 4$ $20x - 30 = 3x + 4$ $17x = 34$ $x = 2$
5	$5 - (2 - x) > 11 - 3x$ $5 - 2 + x > 11 - 3x$ $4x > 8$ $x > 2$	✓	

Solving exponential equations (pp. 53–55)

1 $x = 3$
2 $x = 6$
3 $x = 3$
4 $x = 2$
5 $x = 3$
6 $x = 3$
7 $x = 1$
8 $x = 0$
9 $x = 2$
10 $x = 7$
11 $x = 3$
12 $x = 6$

ISBN: 9780170447096

13 a

Number of hours that have passed (h)	0	1	2	3	4	5	6	7	h
Number of bacteria (b)	1	2	4	8	16	32	64	128	
b expressed as a power of 2	2^0	2^1	2^2	2^3	2^4	2^5	2^6	2^7	2^h

b After one hour there would be three bacteria, and the number would triple during each following hour.

Mixing it up (p. 55)

1 $x = -1$
2 $x = -3$
3 $x \geq 5$
4 $x = 4$
5 $x = 7$
6 $x = -4$
7 $x = 2$
8 $x = 20$
9 $x > 4$
10 $x = 2$
11 $x = -7$
12 $x = -6$

Solving simultaneous equations (pp. 56–62)

1 Substitution (pp. 56–58)

1 $x = 12, y = 4$
2 $x = 6, y = 7$
3 $x = 5, y = 20$
4 $x = 5, y = -3$
5 $x = 10, y = 6$
6 $x = -3, y = 11$
7 $x = 8, y = 7$
8 $x = -9, y = -3$
9 $x = 2y$
$x + y = 39$
$x = 26, y = 13$
Albert has 26 lollies, and Fred has 13.
10 $x = y + 4$
$x + y = 32$
$x = 18, y = 14$
Ana has 18 lollies, and Max has 14.
11 $y = 2x - 3$
$y + 2x = 25$
$x = 7, y = 11$
An adult's ticket costs $11, and a child's ticket costs $7.
12 $y = 2x + 5$
$3y + x = 78$
$x = 9, y = 23$
An adult's ticket costs $23, and a child's ticket costs $9.

2 Elimination (pp. 59–61)

1 $x = 5, y = 4$
2 $x = 2, y = 2$
3 $x = 10, y = 1$
4 $x = 4, y = 7$
5 $x = 2, y = 3$
6 $x = 2, y = 1$
7 $x = 6, y = 2$
8 $x = 9, y = 5$
9 $y + x = 47$
$y - x = 19$
$x = 14, y = 33$
Georgia is 14, and her mum is 33.
10 $y - x = 22$
$x + 2y = 83$
$x = 13, y = 35$
Hemi is 13, and his dad is 35 .
11 $2y - x = 5$
$y + 3x = 13$
$x = 7, y = 11$
A muffin costs $4, and a sandwich costs $3.
12 $3y + 2x = 6.5$
$2y - x = 2$
$x = 1, y = 1.5$
An apple costs $1, and a juicy costs $1.50.

Mixing it up (p. 62)

[1] 1		[2] 7	[3] 2		[4] 2	[5] 4
0			[6] 1	[7] 3		8
[8] 2	2	[9] 5		[10] 1	[11] 2	
		0			[12] 8	[13] 1
[14] 4		[15] 4	3	[16] 2		0
[17] 2	[18] 1			0		
	[19] 1	0		[20] 8	0	0

Challenge 5 (p. 63)

1 Let p represent the price of a carton of popcorn, and i represent the price of an ice cream.
$3p + 2i = 14$ $p - i = 0.50$
Popcorn costs $3 and an ice cream costs $2.50.
2 Let u be the cost to unlock the scooter, and let t be the cost for ten minutes' use.
$2u + 6t = 3.90$ $u = 10t$
The unlock cost is $1.50 and it costs 15c per ten minutes.
3 Let x represent the number.
$\frac{2x - 3}{5} = 39 - 4x$
The number is 9.
4 $\frac{2x - 5}{3} + 2x - 5 = \frac{4(x + 2)}{3}$
$x = 7$
Triangle: 3cm, 4 cm, 5 cm
Square: 3 cm

 ISBN: 9780170447096

Quadratic expressions (pp. 64–71)

Expanding quadratic expressions (pp. 64–65)

1 $x^2 + 6x + 5$ **2** $x^2 + 4x - 21$
3 $x^2 - 8x - 9$ **4** $x^2 - 12x + 32$
5 $x^2 + 14x + 49$ **6** $x^2 - 12x + 36$
7 $x^2 + 0x - 100$ **8** $x^2 + x - 6$
9 $x^2 - 3x - 88$ **10** $x^2 - 5x + 4$
11 $3x^2 + 14x + 8$ **12** $2x^2 + x - 3$
13 $5x^2 - 7x + 2$ **14** $x^2 - 14x + 49$
15 $x^2 - 36$ **16** $2x^2 - 23x - 12$

Factorising quadratic expressions (pp. 66–67)

1 $(x + 11)(x + 1)$ **2** $(x + 2)(x + 4)$
3 $(x + 5)(x - 1)$ **4** $(x + 2)(x - 6)$
5 $(x - 6)(x + 3)$ **6** $(x - 1)(x + 10)$
7 $(x - 8)^2$ **8** $(x + 4)(x - 4)$
9 $(x + 1)(x + 3)$ **10** $(x + 1)(x + 17)$
11 $(x + 1)(x + 6)$ **12** $(x + 2)(x + 3)$
13 $(x - 1)(x - 6)$ **14** $(x - 2)(x - 3)$
15 $(x + 6)(x - 1)$ **16** $(x + 1)(x - 6)$
17 $(x - 2)(x + 3)$ **18** $(x + 2)(x - 3)$
19 $(x + 3)^2$ **20** $(x + 6)^2$
21 $(x - 10)^2$ **22** $(x + 7)(x - 7)$
23 $(x - 9)^2$ **24** $(x + 1)(x - 1)$
25 $(x + 0.1)(x - 0.1)$ **26** $(x - 11)^2$

Solving quadratic equations (pp. 68–71)

1 Factorised quadratic equations

1 $x = -3$ or $x = -7$ **2** $x = -2$ or $x = -5$
3 $x = -3$ or $x = 6$ **4** $x = -1$ or $x = 9$
5 $x = 11$ or $x = -4$ **6** $x = -5$ or $x = 2$
7 $x = -3$ or $x = 7$ **8** $x = 2$ or $x = -6$
9 $x = -4$ or $x = 10$ **10** $x = -7$ or $x = 7$
11 $x = 12$ **12** $x = -4$
13 $x = 8$ **14** $x = 2$ or $x = -2$

2 Unfactorised quadratic equations

1 $x = -1$ or $x = -3$ **2** $x = -2$ or $x = -5$
3 $x = -7$ or $x = 4$ **4** $x = -3$ or $v = 8$
5 $x = -9$ or $x = -4$ **6** $x = -5$ or $x = 11$
7 $x = 2$ or $x = 8$ **8** $x = -4$ or $x = 6$
9 $x = 2$ or $x = 9$ **10** $x = -2$ or $x = 32$
11 $x = 3$ or $x = -7$ **12** $x = 9$ or $x = -4$
13 $x = 7$ or $x = -7$ **14** $x = -8$
15 $x = 0$ or $x = 13$ **16** $x = 4$ or $x = 5$
17 $x = 15$ or $x = -2$ **18** $x = 0$ or $x = -1$

3 Quadratic equations with a common factor

1 $x = -1$ or $x = -5$ **2** $x = 4$ or $x = -4$
3 $x = -1$ or $x = -3$ **4** $x = 3$ or $x = -4$
5 $x = 3$ or $x = 5$ **6** $x = -3$ or $x = 6$
7 $x = 1$ or $x = -1$ **8** $x = -3$

Challenge 6 (p. 72)

1 $x = -\frac{1}{2}$ or $x = -3$ **2** $x = -\frac{2}{3}$ or $x = -1$
3 $x = -\frac{3}{2}$ or $x = -2$ **4** $x = -3$ or $x = -\frac{2}{5}$
5 $x = \frac{1}{2}$ or $x = -3$ **6** $x = -1$ or $x = \frac{2}{3}$
7 $x = 3$ or $x = -\frac{1}{7}$ **8** $x = 5$ or $x = -\frac{1}{3}$
9 $x = 3$ or $x = \frac{1}{2}$ **10** $x = 1$ or $x = \frac{2}{3}$
11 $x = 1$ or $x = \frac{3}{2}$ **12** $x = \frac{1}{2}$ or $x = -\frac{1}{2}$
13 $x = \frac{2}{3}$ or $x = -\frac{2}{3}$ **14** $x = -0.7$ or $x = 0.7$

Find the errors (p. 73)

	✓/✗	Correct solution
1	✗	$5y + 3x = 1$ ① $x = 11 - 7y$ ② Substitute ② into ①: $5y + 3(11 - 7y) = 1$ $5y + 33 - 21y = 1$ $-16y = -32$ ∴ **$y = 2$ and $x = -3$**
2	✗	$2x^2 - 10x - 12 = 0$ $2(x^2 - 5x - 6) = 0$ $2(x + 1)(x - 6) = 0$ ∴ $x = -1$ or $x = 6$
3	✓	
4	✓	
5	✗	$x^2 - 2x - 15 = 0$ $(x + 3)(x - 5) = 0$ ∴ $x = -3$ or $x = 5$

Challenge 7 (p. 74)

[1] 1	2	[2] 1		[3] 3	[4] 5	
		2			[5] 1	[6] 7
		[7] 4	4	[8] 1		2
[9] 5	[10] 6			1		
	[11] 3	[12] 2		[13] 2	4	[14] 2
[15] 4		[16] 2	[17] 5			0
[18] 2	1		[19] 4	8		0

Understanding instructions in algebra (pp. 75–78)

1 Simplify $6p^2 + 7q + 1$
2 Solve $x = 4$
3 Factorise $5xy(x + 4y)$
4 Simplify $\frac{2y^5}{3x}$
5 Solve $x = 7$ or $x = -11$
6 Evaluate -30
7 Solve $x = 5$
8 Solve $x = 3$ or $x = -1$
9 Expand $-2p^3 + 6p^2 + 18p$
10 Evaluate 1.6
11 Solve $x = 4$
12 Solve $x > -2$
13 Expand $30pq^4 - 15p^3q^3$
14 Simplify $12a^5b^4c^2$
15 Solve $x = 4$
16 Factorise $(x + 9)(x - 3)$
17 Solve $x = 4$ or $x = -4$
18 Expand $3x^2 + x - 14$

Revision 1 (pp. 79–81)

1 $\frac{x}{2} - 23$
2 A third of the difference between five and a number.
3 a The variable is **s** and it stands for **the number of students**.
b 92 sausages
4 a $5p^6$ b $6d^4e^5f^5$
c 3 d $3f^2 + f - 3e$
e $\frac{3c^4}{2b}$ f $\frac{a}{3b^4}$
g $20\,000p^{20}$ h 0
5 a $15yz + 10x^2z$ b $6p^2q - 12pq$
6 a $8r(3q + 1)$ b $-3s^2t(5t + 2)$
7

Formula	d = 6, e = 2	d = 3, e = 6	d = –3, e = 4	d = –5, e = –3
$A = de - 3e^2$	$A = 0$	$A = -90$	$A = -60$	$A = -12$

8 a $p = 2$ b $x = 12$
c $x = 2$ d $f = 3$
e $z = -4$ f $x \le 2$
g $x > -1$ h $x = 8$
i $x = 3, y = 7$ j $x = -1, y = 3$
9 a $7 = \frac{3x - 4}{2}$
$x = 6$
b $\frac{x}{4} - 5 = x + 1$
$x = -8$
c $x + (x + 3) + (x + 6) = 45$
The three numbers are 12, 15 and 18.
10 $110 + 12x \ge 360$, $x \ge 20.83$
He needs to work for at least 21 hours.
11 $y = 2x + 0.5$
$4y + 3x = 35$
A drink costs \$3 and a hamburger costs \$6.50.
12 a $2x^2 + 3x - 20$ b $(x - 9)(x + 2)$
c $x = -3$ or $x = 9$ d $x = -4$ or $x = 3$
e $x = -6$ or $x = 6$ f $x = 2$ or $x = 4$
13 a Solve $x = 14$ or $x = -2$
b Evaluate -15

Revision 2 (pp. 82–84)

1 $(y - 5)^2$
2 A third of the difference between double a number and 1.
3 a The variable is **s** and it stands for **the number of students**.
b 12 radios
4 a $6p^7$ b $14a^7b^7$
c 8 d $x^2y - 2xy + 5$
e $\frac{3}{gh}$ f $\frac{1}{4p^2q^5}$
g $144p^{12}$ h $6a$
5 a $28y^3 + 21y$ b $12pq - 4p^3$
6 a $4w(3 + 5v)$ b $3mn(1 - 5m^3n)$
7

Formula	d = 6, e = 2	d = 3, e = 6	d = –3, e = 4	d = –5, e = –3
$A = de - 3e^2$	$A = 30$	$A = -80$	$A = -460$	$A = -48$

8 a $p = 4$ b $x = -4$
c $x = 2$ d $f = -0.6$
e $z = -0.4$ f $x > 2$
g $x \ge 3$ h $x = 5$
i $x = 5, y = -1$ j $x = 7, y = 2$
9 a $\frac{5x - 7}{4} + 1 = x - 2$
$x = -5$
b $\frac{2x}{3} - 7 = x - 12$, $x = 15$
c $x + (x + 2) + (x + 4) - 10 = 53$.
The three numbers are 19, 21 and 23.
10 $4 + 2(r - 1) < 29$, $x < 13.5$.
Maximum number of rows is 13.
11 $x = 2y - 8$
$5x + 4y = 58$
A piece of fish costs \$6 and a cheeseburger costs \$7.
12 a $3x^2 - 5x - 22$ b $(x - 3)(x - 12)$
c $x = -12$ or $x = 7$ d $x = 8$ or $x = 3$
e $x = -5$ f $x = -8$ or $x = 1$
13 a Factorise $(x - 1)(x - 1)$
b Solve $x = 0.5$

ISBN: 9780170447096